IS GOD STILL SPEAKING?

Examining the Relevance of
Modern Prophetic Ministry

IS GOD STILL SPEAKING?

Examining the Relevance of Modern Prophetic Ministry

Kevin E. Winters

Is God Still Speaking?

Examining the Relevancy of Modern Prophetic Ministry

By Kevin E. Winters

Copyright © 2020 by Kevin E. Winters. All rights reserved. This book or parts thereof may not be reproduced in any form, stored in a retrieval system, or transmitted in any form by any means: electronic, mechanical, photocopy, recording, or otherwise, without prior written permission of the publisher, except as provided by United States of America copyright Law.

Published by Kevin E. Winters, 12700 Denny Court, Upper Marlboro MD Kevinewintersministries@gmail.com

International Standard Book Number:
978-0-9977334-6-4

Printed in the United States of America

Cover design and page layout by Artiest Design and Illustration

Unless otherwise indicated, all Scripture quotations are from the Holy Bible, King James Version, New King James Version, or New International Version.

"Scripture taken from the New King James Version and New International Version. Copyright © 1982 by Thomas Nelson, Inc. Used by permission. All rights reserved."

"THE HOLY BIBLE. NEW INTERNATIONAL VERSION®, NIV®, Copywrite © 1973, 1978, 1984, 2011 by Biblica, Inc.™ Used by permission. All rights reserved worldwide"

Dedication

I would like to dedicate this book to the Body of Christ whom I love. I do so considering the great honor the Father has bestowed upon me to share what I believe is a balanced approach to receiving God's messages. Please know that I relish in the idea of serving you, and I am committed to doing so with every ounce of my being.

Last, but most certainly not least, I dedicate this book to the best leader, teacher, and friend in the universe—the Holy Spirit. It is my prayer that the purposes of Your heart are satisfied with every word, paragraph, and chapter of this book.

Acknowledgements

It would be folly for me not to recognize the most important people in my life. First, to my wife. I love you and cherish our years together. It is inspiring watching you evolve from level to level, bravely chasing your dream. I dare to say that it has helped me to grow into the man, husband, and father I am today. Thank you for always being a friend first. I love you to pieces.

Next, I want to acknowledge my children, Autumn, Caleb, Aaron, and Noelle. Thank you for allowing me space to explore God's path for my life. Daddy loves each one of you more than words can describe. Thank you for allowing me to be the best me I can be, even when I seem weird.

Finally, I want to acknowledge all of my followers on the various social media platforms. You have trusted me to speak into your lives, you are as much a part of the formation of this book as anyone else in my life. You often encourage me with your emails and instant messages. Many times, I receive those messages right when I need them. Thank you for hanging in there with me. I pray that this book makes God come alive in your lives and ministries.

PREFACE

I have experienced many wonderful things in my life. Hearing God's voice is at the top of the list. It has led to the most awesome relationship with the Spirit of God. Hearing His voice has also changed my life forever. For instance, His voice rescued me from the consequences of bad educational decisions. Furthermore, it led me into a fruitful career as a graphic designer. His words in my ear have even aided my parenting, resulting in awesome children. It has even guided my ministry, kept me from being swindled, and helped me advise other people. I don't know what I would do if God ever stopped speaking to me.

Today, we unfortunately question the reality and possibility of hearing God's voice. In fact, rejection is a common reaction to those who admit to these types of encounters with God. For that reason, I am compelled to address the matter. First, let me state my main purpose for writing this book. I did not write it to sway anyone to believe what I believe. My sole purpose for this book is to offer a counter argument to the teaching that God no longer speaks to humanity. I want people to walk away armed with enough information to make an informed decision regarding the subject. Consequently, good decisions are the result of being well-informed. No one should make a decision based on a one-sided argument. I very much respect leaders, yet, I do not subscribe to the idea that we are to blindly follow them. While I believe in giving them proper reverence, I also deeply believe in Paul's words to the Thessalonians, *"...test all things. Hold fast to what is good."* Lastly, I wholeheartedly believe in the importance of discernment. Finally, I believe that the rightly divided word of God is the way to get to the truth. I also want you to understand that this book is not a knee-jerk reaction to the subject. Instead, it is a decisive and calculated response to an encounter that beckoned me to write it. In fact, it all started with a debate on social media.

I am a man of many gifts and talents. One of my favorite God-given gifts is writing. I absolutely love to write. I am also a teacher and a prophet. These two gifts work together to fill my inner world with logic and intuition. Working together, through the Holy Spirit, they help to me create insightful teachings. Being a writer also means exposing myself to willing readers. After all, what good is writing if there is no one around to read it. Therefore, I often share my teachings with the world via my blog and various social media platforms. As you might expect, with access to such a vast sea of people, I attract internet trolls. In fact, one particular article titled, K.I.S.S.-Keep It Simple Saints: How we complicate hearing God's voice, attracted one. The article shared five ways that believers complicate the simple process of hearing God's voice. Not long after it posted on Facebook a Christian brother, offended by the article's premise, posted a contrary response to the article. At first, I did not bother to respond. After all, I did post it to a social platform with millions of users. Opposing opinions are common and expected. Some of my readers, however, did not like his response. So, they decided to engage him. Then the man proceeded to post insults directed at a particular person. Some of his insults were accompanied by scripture aimed at justifying his point of view, others were not. As he kept posting, I decided to involve myself in the conversation. I did so because I wanted to fully hear his point of view on the matter of hearing God's voice.

His displeasure with the article centered around his belief that God no longer speaks to mankind. He had been taught that God went silent once the canon of scripture was closed. Furthermore, he was also taught that God only speaks to us by the canonized word, the Bible. His anger toward us grew out of this understanding. Likewise, he assumed that I was blaspheming against the Bible. Therefore, he honestly thought that he was defending it. With that in mind, I allowed him to share what he believed. Then I patiently and calmly responded to the errors in his teaching. After a while, it became clear to him that he could not biblically nor convincingly defend his position, so he stopped posting. As a gesture of Christian brotherly love, I opted to write an article on the subject. I also offered to allow him to read the article. I only asked that he did so with an open mind. Well, here is the article!

At the end of our friendly and spirited debate, I realized that the scriptures and ideas he put forth were common. Everyone opposed to hearing the voice of God always used the same scriptures to justify their point of view. That alerted me to the reality that there is a doctrine behind their belief. So, I found the main espousers of the doctrine and sincerely listened to their perspective on the matter. Then I concluded that an article was not a suitable outlet for addressing this complex subject. I realized that I needed to do something substantial. I had to write a book. Therefore, I took on the challenge of using the Bible to debunk the most popular ideas in the teaching. I also thought it would be wise to clear up any misunderstandings as it relates to prophecy. To do so I took an honest look at the fears that keep people from believing that they can hear from God. I also looked at the failures and rouge prophetic practices that contribute to that fear. Finally, I wrote out biblical suggestions to help Christians safely incorporate the voice of God into their lives.

I believe this book is the answer to the question, "Is God still speaking?" After reading it, I hope that you feel the same.

Happy reading!

Table of Contents

Introduction
1 Is God Still Speaking?

Chapter 1
5 The Voice of God as Scripture

Chapter 2
15 The Prophetic Voice of God

Chapter 3
33 The Relationship Between God's Written and Spoken Word

Chapter 4
41 The Divine Communication Hierarchy

Chapter 5
59 Common Arguments Against Hearing God's Voice

Chapter 6
137 Addressing Our Fear of Deception

Chapter 7
177 Addressing a Specific Fear

Chapter 8
205 The Unchanging God

Chapter 9
209 One Last Thing

216 About the Author

218 Resources

Introduction

Is God Still Speaking?

One of the biggest arguments in the Church today surrounds the subject of hearing the voice of God. On one side, there are those who believe that God is still speaking to us. On the other side, there are those vehemently opposed to the idea. Those in opposition believe that the era of God speaking directly to humanity ended with the canonization of the scriptures. This group also views those who claim to hear from God as heretics. Some of them even go as far as calling them delusional and deceived. In addition, they charge them with devaluing the Bible. Somehow, they concluded that the word of God and the voice of God cannot coexist, or at least not in this era.

To be fair, they have legitimate concerns. It is no secret that experiences such as seeing visions, following dreams, and hearing voices have led to some extreme things, such as the establishment of the Mormon Church, Islam, and Christian Science, amongst others. We also know that some serial killers and extremists such as Osama Bin Laden, Timothy McVey, David Koresh, and most famously Charles Mansion, attributed their actions to such experiences. For that reason, I understand their apprehension. Nonetheless, a few bad experiences spawned by supernatural spiritual communication, account for only a few of the issues in today's Church. In fact, there are more good stories about hearing the voice of God than there are bad ones. Of course, those opposed choose to focus on the hurtful experiences rather than the awesome testimonies of those who benefited from their encounter with God.

Today's Church has many challenges. There is rampart sexual sin, a lack of ministerial integrity among the clergy, thievery, racism, and most notably—separatism. While these challenges plague congregations around the world, few of them are the result of a supernatural experience. Separatism, for instance, is almost exclusively rooted in on going debates about the written word.

It is no secret that the Church is divided. Personally, I find it to be a tad bit strange considering that there are so many scripture references to God's call for oneness. Paul encourages the Corinthians to be of one mind (2 Cor. 13:11). James, contending for the unity of the Church, challenges our relationship with fellow humans (James 4:11-12). Lastly, Jesus prayed for us that we would be "one" (John 17:20-23). Yet, we are vastly divided.

In preparing to write this book, I googled the word "de-

Introduction

nominations." The results were stunning. I always believed that there were no more than seven. I was wrong! The results showed that there are thousands of denominations. Yes, I said thousands! Moreover, again, I remind you that most denominations are not the result of supernatural revelations of some kind. Instead, they are the direct outgrowth of doctrinal disagreements regarding the written word. So, while it is true that supernatural revelation can lead to deception, it is also true that the misinterpretation of the written word can cause deception and damage to the Body of Christ. I do not make this point to shame anyone. I make it to highlight the fact that we are human. I also want to note that there is no full proof method that insulates us from deception.

Therefore, as one who has watched this argument take shape over the years, I thought it would be wise to take an honest look at the debate. Let me say upfront, that I am going to argue that God is still speaking to us. Though this is my intent, I am also going to look at the argument against it realistically. It would be unfair to ignore the legitimate fears some harbor regarding the matter. Moreover, as I stated before, there are genuine fears to address.

Finally, though I intend to make a case for the acceptance of prophetic gifting in today's church, I am also purposing to build that case from the written word. I intend to prove that the existence of the Bible does not exclude the need for prophecy and vice versa. Furthermore, I do not know a rational believer that can say that they hear the voice of God and denounce His written word. I believe it is the ultimate authority in the life of the true believer. I also believe, however, that there are moments in our life when God finds it necessary to speak to us directly. Likewise, I plan to make that case by exploring the most regarded misunderstandings about hearing God's voice.

Chapter 1

The Voice of God as Scripture

The Bible is the voice of God. Grounding us in the validity of scripture's authority is the right place to start when addressing this argument. It is hardly a challenge to ignore someone who dares to say that the scriptures are not the voice of God. I have never seen nor met one Christian that reduced the Bible to a mere book. Sometimes, the argument regarding hearing the voice of God is based on the fact that there are people who think that prophecy supersedes the written word. Now, while I have never met a Christian who regards the scriptures as invalid, I have met plenty of them that have elevated something they believed God spoke to them, over what He wrote to us all. That behavior partly fuels the argument from those who oppose hearing the voice of God.

We even have relatively recent examples of people exalting the voice of God over the written word of God. One such example comes from a former general in the Pentecostal Church. This man heard a voice say something that contradicted scriptures, justified it as truth by his logic, and acted on it. The result was the creation of a different and dangerous version of Christianity. Likewise, his spiritual demise has been slow but steady. He went from spearheading Pentecostal truths, walking in miracles, casting out demons, healing the sick, and walking in purity, to loose living, and denying that demons even exist. Again, it is examples like his that make so many Christian leaders leery of those who claim to hear from God. Moreover, I completely understand their hesitancy.

In light of this preacher's unfortunate travesty, we must make the right assessment of his error. Some who know his story attribute his mistake to the voice he heard. They say, "This would not have happened had he just allowed the scriptures to speak in his life, and not some voice." I, however, would like to submit a different point of view. I do not believe his error was hearing a voice. I believe that his mistake was his view of the scriptures. I think it is apparent that he believes in a hierarchy of spiritual communication.

Whether conscious or unconscious, many people inappropriately believe in a hierarchy of divine communication. Some suppose that a message from an angel carries more weight than one from a preacher. Others assume that a message from a vision is more valuable than an *inner* impression. There are also those who regard the opinion of their pastor over the Bible. Lastly, there are those who believe that any divine experience is more significant than something we might glean from the scriptures. Again, some of this is done consciously. Other times, it is unconsciously done; nonetheless, it happens quite often.

It is, in fact, the reason why we have some of our cultic sects of Christianity. These cults, as well as the errors of others, are the offspring of those who gave people, things, and experiences a higher place value than the Bible. That explains why the preacher can live a lifestyle of sin and keep preaching. That is why the prophet can speak contrary to the scriptures and still grow a following. That is why we follow people into poverty every other year on the word that they have a unique insight into the day of Jesus' return. These things happen because we do not see the value of God's written word. I will say more about this subject in chapter four.

Lest I seem one-sided, even those who champion the idea of "the closed canon," often live in opposition to it. I'll prove some of that later in this book. I have been around the Church all of my life. Over the years, I have seen many people take extreme positions on various issues. One thing I noticed is that even those against the belief that God speaks directly to us, ignore the written word when it contradicts their desires. As a result, we have more divorces, more pulpit pimps and child molesters, more adulterers, more fornicators, more everything. Why are there so many difficulties among people who claim to read their Bibles regularly? Whether you believe God is still speaking or not, you must have as your base, a commitment to the scriptures. They must be ground zero! This truth must be non-negotiable in the believer's life.

Knowing What He Said Before

I am one that teaches people how to hear and recognize the voice of God. Likewise, the most important thing that I teach is this; "The key to knowing what God *is saying* is knowing what God *has said*." That is the thought that I desperately try to get across to those who desire to hear God's voice. That means that we need to accept, as truth, that the written word is, in fact, a vehicle of the actual voice of God. Recognizing this is the foundation to monitoring and discerning our supernatural encounters with voices, dreams, and visions.

Sometimes, I marvel at where we are today as the Body of Christ. We have so much at our fingertips that the early Church did not possess. We have a complete Bible, Old, and New Testament. The early Church only had the Old Testament. We have their testimonies and examples captured in ink. We can study what the early church did, how they did it, where they went wrong, how it affected them, and the proper way to do things. They had no examples to follow. We even have special study tool like topical Bibles that group together all related passages of scripture. We have every single thing we need to be successful. Still, we have more people who hate church than at any time in its history. We have more sick and demonized people. We have more understanding and less result from that understanding. We have the written word and do not value the fact that it points to a God that speaks. Ultimately, God made His thoughts available to us, but we do not appreciate this reality.

God's View of His Word

I think that the way to resolve this issue is to get us back to honoring the voice of God in all its various forms, not esteeming one over the other. I also believe that we first need to start by looking at how God views His written word. Deuteronomy 28:1-2 reads:

> "Now it shall come to pass, if you **obey the voice of the Lord your God**, to observe carefully all of **His commandments** which I command you today, that the Lord your God will set you high above all the nations of the earth. And all these blessings shall come upon you and overtake you because you **obey the voice of the Lord.**"

Notice the bolded parts of the text. God says that the blessings available to Israel would only come by obedience to His voice. What does the word voice refer to in the passage? Was He referring to the spoken word or the written word? In the context of this passage, He was referring to the written word of God. So, we can conclude that God equates the commandments in the law to His voice. Israel was to always regard these written words as though spoken in the present tense. These written words were to be the balance by which they weighed their actions. They taught them how to eat, dress, treat each other, treat their neighbor, how to deal with foreigners, how to raise their children, respect their parents, deal with debtors, sacrifices for sin, how to worship, what not to worship, how to hear from God, how to recognize His prophetic word, and more. In other words, there was no shortage of content. God made sure to cover every single aspect of the life He expected them to live.

Not only did God provide them with a written form of instruction. He also expected them to refer to it regularly. Deuteronomy 6:1-8 reads:

> *These are the commands, decrees and laws the Lord your God directed me to teach you to observe in the land that you are crossing the Jordan to possess, so that you, your children and their children after them may fear the Lord your God as long as you live by keeping all his decrees and commands that I give you, and so that you may enjoy long life. Hear, Israel, and be careful to obey so that it may go well with you and that you may increase greatly in a land flowing with milk and honey, just as the Lord, the God of your ancestors, promised you. Hear, O Israel: The Lord our God, the Lord is one. Love the Lord your God with all your heart and with all your soul and with all your strength. These commandments that I give you today are to be on your hearts. Impress them on your children. Talk about them when you sit at home and when you walk along the road, when you lie down and when you get up. Tie them as symbols on your hands and bind them on your foreheads.*

Deuteronomy 11:18 also carries the same idea of living by God's written word. It reads:

Fix these words of mine in your hearts and minds; tie them as symbols on your hands and bind them on your foreheads.

He also expected the leaders to teach it. (See Deut. 6:1 and Ezra 7:10 for examples).

These passages provide us with a strong sense that the Bible is God's voice. Paul likewise confirms this to his spiritual son Timothy. He says in 2 Timothy 3:16:

"All scripture is given by inspiration of God, and is profitable for doctrine, for reproof, for correction, for instruction in righteousness."

Here again, we see the idea that we are to wholeheartedly embrace God's written word. The word inspired in this passage means *"God-breathed."* It tells us that God Himself gave the authors the words He wanted to be penned. That alone puts the Bible into an entirely different category. Most other literary, religious works came about via human intervention. Moreover, those who adhere to these writings acknowledge that a man, whether Buddha, or Mohammed, or Confucius, wrote them. They also believed that their words were the outgrowth of special revelations gained by their human pursuits. Our faith, however, differs because 2 Peter 1:21 says that prophecy did not come by the will *(efforts)* of man, but holy men of God spoke as they were moved *(inspired)* to speak.

This understanding tells us that we can trust God's word. It is a completed work that addresses our every concern. Whether Old or New Testament, it discusses everything; how we dress, what we eat, healing *(supernatural and natural)*, deliverance, forgiveness, how to treat others, how to manage our finances, and more. Understanding this is essential to understanding the rest of this book. Interestingly enough, the written word of God also addresses how to know when God is speaking directly to us! As I said before, the key to knowing what God is saying is knowing what God has already said.

The Best Example in Scripture

When I think of how God views His word, Joshua comes to mind. In my opinion, his story sums up this subject better than any other in the Bible. Look at God's words to the newly appointed leader of Israel.

> *"Be strong and very courageous. Be careful to obey all the law my servant Moses gave you; do not turn from it to the right or to the left, that you may be successful wherever you go. Keep this Book of the Law always on your lips; meditate on it day and night, so that you may be careful to do everything written in it. Then you will be prosperous and successful. (Joshua 1:7-8, NIV)*

The Voice of God as Scripture

Wow! That is powerful. Joshua's success was completely dependent upon his respect and faith in God's written word. God even encouraged his obedience by using some rather strong terminology. He said to him, *"Be careful to obey..."* The word "careful" means to be diligent, attentive, or conscientious. I believe the truth of this passage is paramount. So many believers look to this passage as the blueprint for success. I certainly do! Its example is clear; God's written word is the key to life. I can wholeheartedly say that leaning on the scriptures has produced a great number of exciting victories in my life. I am sure that you can say the same as well.

One of my favorite scriptures reads:

"Wisdom is the principle thing, in all your getting get understanding." (Proverbs 4:7, NKJV)

I live by these words. I apply them to both my secular and spiritual life. Likewise, I have watched God take me from the file room to be the lead graphic designer in my agency. And He did so even though I did not have a formal education beyond high school. The key to my success was my application of Proverbs 4:7. It was my aggressive stance towards making myself knowledgeable about my craft, with or without access to traditional education. It was my willingness to adhere to God's word to Joshua. I was careful to do what was in His written word and it produced the success I desired.

Yes, the scriptures are God's voice to humanity. Yes, we need them to guide our decisions, counsel us in times of need, and structure a path of righteousness. It is folly to disregard them, and unwise to cast them away.

Let me end this chapter the same way I started it: The scriptures are the voice of God!

2
Chapter

The Prophetic Voice of God

While I certainly love the scriptures, I cannot ignore the unmistakable truth that God has the ability to speak. The book of Hebrews opens with these words:

> "God, who at various times and various ways spoke in times past to the fathers by the prophets..." (Heb. 1:1, NKJV)

This passage speaks of a quality in which God often relished. Over and over, God distinguishes Himself from false gods by the fact that He is a God that hears and speaks. Look at what Psalm 115:4-7 says:

But their idols are silver and gold, made by human hands. They have mouths, **but cannot speak***, eyes, but cannot see. They have ears, but cannot hear, noses, but cannot smell. They have hands, but cannot feel, feet, but cannot walk,* **nor can they utter a sound with their throats**

Also read Jer. 10:3-5.

"...for the customs of the peoples are futile; For one cuts a tree from the forest, The work of the hands of the workman, with the ax. They decorate it with silver and gold; They fasten it with nails and hammers So that it will not topple. They are upright, like a palm tree, And **they cannot speak***; They must be carried, Because they cannot go by themselves. Do not be afraid of them, For they cannot do evil, Nor can they do any good."*

It does not take a biblical genius to understand the value of God opening His mouth. It was by opening His mouth that He created the worlds. It was with those words that He commanded the waters to divide from the land. It was His voice that delivered Moses from a life of mediocrity. It was His spoken word that brought liberty to Israel. We serve a God that speaks, and I am so glad that He does.

We should also note that it is the very Bible that we hold so dear that teaches us that He speaks. One thing the Bible says, that is often taken out of context, is that the scriptures are good for doctrine. Today we apply that to the whole canon of scripture. Most people, however, don't seem to realize to which scriptures Paul is referring. When Paul makes this statement, he does so as he is writing to Timothy. That means that he was not referring to the New Testament scriptures. After all, he was in the process of unknowingly writing them at the time. Therefore, understanding this passage requires us to unveil the immediate interpretation. The immediate interpretation is the idea the author intends to communicate to the specific audience he is addressing. To get the immediate application, which refers to how the author's instructions were to be used by those the letter addressed, you must keep the passage in context. If kept in context, we see that Paul is saying that the books of the law and the prophets are good for doctrine. Notice that he does not say that they are good "as" doctrine but good "for" doctrine. In other words, Paul was telling Timothy that those Old Testament scriptures are useful for extracting good truth that we can apply to our life.

Paul mimics this idea in his writing to the Corinthian church. After giving them a very brief history lesson, he makes this statement, *"Now these things became our examples, to the intent that we should not lust after evil things as they also lusted" (1 Cor. 10:1-5,6, NKJV).* Again, Paul is using the Old Testament scriptures as the foundation for his conclusion.

Prophecy

That leads us to the example that some seem to want to ignore. God has left us many illustrations of Him speaking. It is called prophecy. Prophecy is God speaking directly to a person to share His thoughts, ideas, and plans. Some limit it to talking about the future. That conclusion is drawn in part from our understanding of the New Testament use of the word. The Greek word for prophecy is "propheteia." It means foretelling. It is only used in a few places in the New Testament. (See 1 Cor. 12:10 and Romans 12:6.) The Old Testament word, however, presents a more substantial definition. The Hebrew word for prophet is "nabi." It means to bubble up or forth, to speak as an oracle or an inspired speaker. As you can see, to get a good understanding of the role of prophecy, you need both contexts.

There are many Old and New Testament examples of this gift in operation; most notably in 2 Kings. In this passage, the prophet Elisha was called upon to prophesy to two kings. When he arrived, he immediately realized that Ahab, a king he despised, was present. Ahab's presence sparked indignation in the heart of the man of God. He even went so far as telling the king to go to his mother's false prophets for a word. If that were not enough, he then said to him that he would not speak to him or look at him if it were not for the king he regarded, Jehoshaphat. Then the scriptures showed us how God inspired the prophets' messages. 2 King 3:15 reads:

> "He said bring me a musician and when the musician played the hand of the Lord came upon him."

We also have a New Testament example of the prophetic in action. One of the last things Jesus told the disciples, before going to the cross was how to handle ministry opportunities. He said in Matthew 10:18-20:

You will be brought before governors and kings for My sake, as a testimony to them and to the Gentiles. But when they deliver you up, do not worry about how or what you should speak. For it will be given to you in that hour what you should speak; for it is not you who speak, but the Spirit of your Father who speaks in you.

Then in Acts 2, we see Jesus' words in action when Peter preaches the first sermon. Some have never made the connection between these two passages but Acts 2 is the fulfillment of Matthew 10:18-20. Then it happened again in Act 4:8 when they are arrested. It reads:

"Then Peter, filled with the Holy Spirit, said to them..."

This passage is an example of the prophetic in action.

The Prophetic Nature of the Gospel

Here is something else a lot of people do not realize. The gospel is a "prophetic" message. 2 Peter 1:19 reads:

"And so we have the prophetic word confirmed..."

To understand what Peter is referring to, you have to start reading at verses 16 and 17. In these verses, Peter recounts what he, James, and John experienced with Jesus on the Mount of Transfiguration (Matt. 17:1-13). Remember, it was during this mountain top experience that Jesus was gloriously unveiled before their eyes. They also saw Him speak with Moses and Elijah. However, the experience to which 1 Peter addresses was the part when the glory cloud overshadowed them, and God spoke to them about Jesus; It was the moment when God said, "This is My Beloved Son, hear Him," that Peter refers to as the prophetic word.

The book of Revelation likewise shares this sentiment. Revelation 19:10 says:

> "The spirit of prophecy is the testimony of Jesus Christ."

In other words, the preaching of the gospel is a prophetic display whereby we are empowered by the Holy Spirit to declare Jesus is Lord. 1 Corinthians 12:3, says, speaking about those who speak on God's behalf:

> "No one speaking by the Spirit of God calls Jesus accursed."

Referencing Jesus' spokesman, He also said:

> "And no one can say that Jesus is Lord except **by the Holy Spirit.**"

Finally, Paul presents the idea of the prophetic nature of the Gospel to the Thessalonians. Look at what he writes to them in 1 Thessalonians 2:13.

"For this reason, we also thank God without ceasing, because when you received the word of God which you heard from us, **you welcomed it not as the word of men, but as it is in truth, the word of God,** *which also effectively works in you who believe."*

With this in mind, it is unthinkable to consider the gift of prophecy to be an invalid expression in the Church today. The scriptures we just looked at are clear that prophecy, at its very basis, is the declaration of the Gospel of Jesus Christ. That means that every time we share the Gospel of Jesus Christ with someone, we are speaking prophetically. It also means that every time you share the Gospel with someone, they are hearing the voice of God through you.

The Broader Context

Since we are sharing about the prophetic, I need to clarify something. Many do not realize that there is a difference between "prophecy" and a "prophetic" word. The term prophecy refers to a type of word from God. It is God using His voice to foretell the future. The term prophetic, however, is an attribute of God speaking. For instance, foretelling is a type of word God may speak to us, and the Gospel is another type of word from the mouth of God. So while prophecy is one type of word, there are many different types of prophetic expressions.

If we dig deep into this subject, we see the vastness of the prophetic word. Again, the presentation of the gospel and foretelling are two of many expressions of the prophetic word. For instance, Moses' first word to the Pharaoh was not a foretelling word but a directive word. This teaches us that sometimes, God speaks to us to give us specific instructions. Again, the scriptures are full of such examples. Here are some examples of the kinds of prophetic words God may give us.

Foretelling Words - Foretelling words are those that reveal the future. Daniel and John both had revelations of the future. Elisha in 2 Kings 7:1-2 told the king the exact details of the future economy of Israel. Agabus foretold a coming earthquake in Acts 11:28.

Destiny Words - Destiny words are closely related to foretelling words. God uses them to unveil our design and the work He has called us to do. Foretelling words differ from destiny words in that foretelling words reveal events in the future, whereas destiny words disclose God's future plans for the life of individuals, churches, and organizations. Destiny words in the scriptures are plentiful. Here are a few examples:

- God spoke directly to Moses. (See Exodus 3:7-10.)
- Samuel prophesied the destiny of Saul. (See 1 Samuel 9:27-10:1.)
- Agabus gave Paul and a specific word about his life's work. (See Acts 9:15, 26:15-18.)

- Jeremiah, Isaiah, and Ezekiel received destiny words. (See Jeremiah 1:4-10; Isaiah 1:13; Ezekiel 2:1-10, 3:1-27.)
- The angel Gabriel shared a destiny word about John the Baptist and Jesus. (See Luke 1:11-17 and Luke 1:26-33.)
- Simeon prophesied a destiny word over baby Jesus. (See Luke 2:25-32.)

Words of Wisdom – Words of wisdom are words that advise or give guidance. We see this type of word in many places in the scriptures. In 2 Kings 3:1-19 Elisha tells the kings what to do to win the war. Another great example of words of wisdom at work is visible in Gideon's life. In Judges 7:1-15, God advises him on how to use 300 men to defeat an army. My last example occurs in the life of Jacob in Genesis 30:25-31, 31:1-21. In this story, God advises Jacob on how to increase his gains in light of being cheated by his father-in-law.

Words of Knowledge – Words of knowledge are words from God that inform us in some way. Words of knowledge can materialize as facts about people, places, and things. They can also manifest as supernatural knowledge about subject matters. We see them in many passages of scripture. Ananias received precise information regarding Saul's whereabouts and condition in Acts 9:11-19. We see a similar example in Elisha's life. In 1 Kings 6:8-23, God reveals to him the plans of the King of Assyria. His job was to pass that information to the king of Israel so that He could avoid an ambush. In Daniel's life, we see one of the most incredible demonstrations of this type of word from God. It was through this manifestation that God revealed to Daniel every detail of King Nebuchadnezzar's dream.

As it relates to subject matter words of knowledge, we see it most often in Paul's ministry. Over and over again, we see Paul introducing knowledge that he presumably received via God. He had "subject matter" words of knowledge. That means that God spoke to him about various subjects.

He said in 1 Corinthians 13:2:

"Even though I have the gift of prophecy and **understand all mysteries and all knowledge***..."*

Paul had access to knowledge that was supernaturally imparted. The communion passage in 1 Corinthians 11:23 is a great example of this gift in Paul's ministry. It reads:

"For I received from the Lord that which I also delivered to you; that the Lord Jesus on the same night in which He was betrayed took bread, and when He had given thanks, He broke it..."

How did Paul know what happened that night? He was not there. Verse 23 tells us how, "**For I received from the Lord...**" This is an example of subject matter words of knowledge.

Finally, we also see it in the life of Moses. Read Exodus

34:27. These verses detail Moses receiving the Ten Commandments. This is an awesome example of God giving a man supernatural knowledge.

Directive Words – Directive words are those that tell us to do something. Again, we find such examples in the story of Moses and Pharaoh. God's message to Pharaoh, "Let My people go!" was a directive word. We also see directive words in the life of Philip and Peter. In Acts 8:29, God tells Philip to go near and overtake a chariot. In Acts 10:19-20, God tells Peter that two men are at the door and to go with them asking nothing. The most popular directive word was given to Abraham. In Genesis 22:2, God told him to sacrifice his son, his only begotten son, on a mountain.

Judgment Words – Judgment words are words from God, whereby God charges us with sin. Judgment words reveal the penalty for our actions. We see examples of judgment words spoken against Tyre and Sidon in Isaiah 23. One of the most famous examples of judgment words occurs in the ministry of Jonah. Jonah told the Ninevites that God was going to destroy them in 40 days. Lastly, the prophetic books are filled with examples of judgment words.

Warning Words – Warning words are those that inform us about impending danger. Sometimes that warning lets us know that God is planning to judge us. Other times they appear as words that make us aware of unseen hazards. Warning words are great examples of the mercy of God. We see an example of such in the life of King Abimelech *(Read Genesis chapter 20)*. God spoke to him in a dream and informed him that he was about to commit a sin. He also warned that the resulting sin would bring divine judgment into his life. In God's mercy, He spoke intending to give the king a choice to do right. Nebuchadnezzar's first dream was a warning dream *(Read Daniel chapter 2)*. It warned him that His pride was going to cost him the throne. Jezebel is another excellent example of warning words. In Revelation 2:18-29, God warns a woman named Jezebel to repent of her actions before He passes judgment on her.

Again, sometimes, warning words appear as words that inform us of impending danger. An angel appeared to Joseph, Jesus' stepdad warning him to flee persecution by traveling to Egypt (Matt. 2:13). An angel also warned the wise men not to return to their country (Matt. 2:11-12). God spoke to Elisha so that he could warn the king not to take a particular route (2 Kings 6:8-10).

Encouraging Words – Encouraging words are those words that God speaks to us to give us relief from fear. There is an excellent example of this in Acts 18:9. In this verse of scripture, the Lord encourages the Apostle Paul to speak boldly in His name. He did so by informing him that the many Christians in the city would protect him from the city residents that wanted to harm him.

One of the most popular examples of encouraging words

comes from the book of Joshua. Once God replaced Moses with Joshua, He told him over and over again, "I will be with you" and "do not fear" (See Joshua 1: 6,7,9).

Corrective Words – Corrective words are meant to straighten out our point of view. When Jonah failed to see God's merciful act of withholding judgment, God spoke to him a few times. Each time, He attempted to correct Jonah's attitude.

Blessing Words – The word blessing means to bind to good fortune. In other words, God uses these types of words to speak well or favorable about something or someone. His intent is always to use blessing words to bestow His goodness upon something or someone. We have good examples of these types of words. The most recognizable one comes from the ministry of Balaam (See Numbers 22-24). Many people regard him as a false prophet. However, the scriptures do not reflect that reality. In fact, his story shows us that he had a relationship with God. His problem was not speaking false words, but his willingness to leverage his relationship with God for money.

Blessing words are unique. Their substance is often so ordinary that it is easy to disregard their prophetic nature. That being the case, I want us to closely examine this type of word.

One thing you will notice in Balaam's prophecies is the lack of any grandiose predictions. There was nothing unique about them. If it were not for the scriptures informing us that God spoke to Balaam, we might assume the words are from the prophet instead of God. Look at what he says:

> *"And he took up his oracle and said:*
> *"Balak the king of Moab has brought me from Aram,*
> *From the mountains of the east. 'Come, curse Jacob*
> *for me, and come, denounce Israel!' "How shall I*
> *curse whom God has not cursed? And how shall I*
> *denounce whom the Lord has not denounced? For from*
> *the top of the rocks I see him, and from the hills I behold*
> *him; There! A people dwelling alone, not reckoning itself*
> *among the nations. "Who can count the dust of Jacob,*
> *or number one-fourth of Israel? Let me die the death of*
> *the righteous, and let my end be like his!" (Num. 23:7-10,*
> *NKJV)*

Look at the simple nature of Balaam's prophecy. Also, note that verse 11 identifies this type of prophetic word as a blessing. It reads:

> *"Then Balak said to Balaam, "What have you done to*
> *me? I took you to curse my enemies, and look, you have*
> **blessed them** *bountifully!" (Num. 23: 11, NKJV)*

Then Balaam justifies these words as words from the mouth of God. Look at his response in verse 12:

> *"So he answered and said, "Must I not take heed to speak*

what the LORD has put in my mouth?" (Num. 23:12, NKJV)

I believe that these are the types of words God releases over us during the ministry of laying on of hands. There is an example of such in 1 Timothy 4:14. In this passage, Paul discusses the gift bestowed upon Timothy by himself and the presbytery. I believe these were words of blessing over his future. We even have clear examples of prophetic words manifesting as blessing words in the life of Israel's patriarchs. For instance, Joseph blessed his children, by speaking favorably about their future (See Genesis 48). Isaac also blessed Jacob (See Genesis 27:27-29). Finally, Jacob also blessed his 12 sons (See Genesis 49:1-28).

My final example comes from the life of Mary, the mother of Jesus, and Elizabeth, the mother of John the Baptist. Their example is a modest one. It is found in Luke 1:39-45. This passage details Mary's visit with Elizabeth. At the time, these two women are both pregnant with these great miracle men. The scriptures record that Mary's entrance into the house caused the baby in Elizabeth's womb to jump with excitement. The baby's response to the presence of the Savior also caused a secondary spiritual experience for Elizabeth. In her enthusiasm she was suddenly filled with the Spirit of God. Then being filled with the Spirit of God caused her to speak forth blessing words over Mary. Let's look at this.

"And it happened, when Elizabeth heard the greeting of

Mary, that the babe leaped in her womb; and Elizabeth was filled with the Holy Spirit. Then she spoke out with a loud voice and said, **"Blessed are** *you among women, and blessed* **is** *the fruit of your womb! But why is this granted to me, that the mother of my Lord should come to me? For indeed, as soon as the voice of your greeting sounded in my ears, the babe leaped in my womb for joy.* **Blessed is** *she who believed, for there will be a fulfillment of those things which were told her from the Lord." (Luke 1:41-45, NKJV)*

There are some incredible nuggets in this story. For instance, though trivial sounding, these words are prophetic. Some people may not see the prophetic nature of her words. So, let me show you. First, we know that her words were inspired by God because the Bible tells us. Second, Elizabeth verbal expression contained revelatory information. Notice her words in verse 45. How does she know about Mary's willingness to believe the message that the angel gave her? She states this in contradiction to her husband's unwillingness to believe the message the angel gave him. Next, how did she know that Mary was carrying the Christ child? That information was only given to Mary. Furthermore, scripture does not tell us that Mary divulged that information to anyone. Do you see it now?

At first glance, it is easy to dismiss these types of prophetic words. Our examples show us that sometimes God speaks simplistically. That simplicity may appear as a very informal verbal description of God's favor toward us.

I believe that blessing words are valuable and important. Likewise, they are a huge part of my daily life. I love blessing words. I love them so much that I release them over my family daily.

As you can see, the word of God takes many forms. Likewise, not one of them is without reason or necessity. Later in this book, I will highlight the importance of this information.

Noting these various forms of prophetic expression lends credence and value to God's prophetic voice. We cannot afford to overlook its vastness. Doing so undervalues the role of the Holy Spirit in helping to navigate the believer's life. It also undermines His assignment to help us perform the most basic charge from Jesus, sharing the gospel of Jesus Christ with our fellow man. Two of the most commonly asked questions regarding evangelism are; "How do we approach people, and what do we say?" While the first question may remain a problem for many, the second is not for the person who acknowledges the power of a vocal God.

As I conclude, I want us to agree that the scriptures are the voice of God. There is no debating the matter, and nothing can negate that reality. Likewise, prophecy is not a substitute for the Bible. Instead, it is a multifaceted tool that the scriptures depict as God's way to share His thoughts with us. Finally, to become potent Christians, we must acknowledge that God's voice is both needed and available today, in both variations.

3
Chapter

The Relationship Between God's Written and Spoken Word

There is a misunderstanding that I want to address. Somehow, Christians today believe preachers interact with the written word in a way that is unique to this era. It is the understanding of some people that the prophets of old operated with little regard for the written word. However, that is not true. Just as preachers today speak messages from the basis of the written word, so did the prophets. Though I am doubtful that they preached passages after exegeting them, I am sure that they were careful to know the law. Knowing the law ensured that their prophecy was consistent with God's expressed intent. As I said earlier, you must know what God has said, to know what God is saying!

Prophesying According to the Written Word

When reading the Bible, it is often easy to make assumptions. We somehow fail to consider that we have the luxury of reading about past events. Therefore, we look at the scriptures in a very broad way. When reading about God's interaction with the prophets, we suppose that they heard him audibly, even though most passages are quiet regarding how the prophets actually heard God's voice; we presume that every prophet heard God the way Moses did at the burning bush. We also assume that the word of the Lord through the prophets was not measured against the written standard. However, false prophets were easily identified by their lack of prophetic integrity. False prophet's prophetic words were always noted as being misaligned with the revealed (written laws) word of God.

Look at what Jeremiah 23:15 says:

> *"Also I have seen a horrible thing in the prophets of Jerusalem: They commit adultery and walk in lies;*
> **They also strengthen the hands of evildoers,**
> **So that no one turns back from his wickedness***.*
> *All of them are like Sodom to Me, And her inhabitants like Gomorrah."*

When reading the Bible, we think of the prophet's revelations as profound insights. Most of the time, we make this assumption based on the method whereby the revelation was received. We read about Ezekiel's grand visions and say,

"Wow!" But, when you take the time to read God's recorded words, they were consistent with the law. In our minds, the prophets were God's tools for receiving new revelation. Moreover, to a degree, we glean a lot from what they said. Their words and ideas revealed major themes and concepts about God. Those revelations are the basis for our Christian faith. It was through Isaiah that we learned that God's thoughts are not like our thoughts (Isa. 55:8-9). It was through Moses, Miriam, and Aaron, that we learned that God speaks to prophets in dreams, visions, and dark sayings (Num. 12:6-8). It was through Ezekiel that we learned about the various kinds of angelic beings (Ezek. 1:1-28). However, in the end, these are just glimpses into more significant ideas. When we look at the context of their sermons, and not only the contents, we see a few themes. First, we see the theme that God judges those who break His laws. We also see the idea of a redeeming and loving God. That is the gist of every one of their sermons; while the details may change regarding who, what, when, where, and why, the context often remained the same.

Genuine preachers understand what I am saying. I have taken four preaching classes over the last twenty years. During that time, I have seen the vastness of the Bible. I have witnessed 12 preachers preach the same passage of scripture 12 different ways. To reach their conclusions, they each had access to the same words, characters, and everything in between. Yet, somehow, each saw the passage differently. Likewise, that difference was visible when they executed their thoughts about the text. Even with all of those distinct points of view, they concluded that the one passage centered around one central idea. While the details were dissimilar, the fundamental concept of the message was the same.

When we look at the passages preached by the prophets of old, we need to keep in mind that God communicates an idea, not just details. For instance, Jeremiah was not preaching a revelation of a coming judgment. God was very clear, in the 28th chapter of Deuteronomy that serving other gods would result in their demise. The revelation unveiled whom God would use, how much time was involved, and by what means they would suffer. In fact, one of the things that angered God so often about the false prophets is that they preached peace and prosperity to an Israel that was serving other gods. Israel's actions conflicted with the written word of God. How then was it possible for them to prosper? See, the false prophets led people away from God by prophesying "outside" of the written word.

The same is true today. We know something is from God when it operates in harmony with what He wrote to us. This principle is true in all aspects of our life. Regardless of how we use this principle, we are all required to allow our lives, decisions, and ways to line up with the written word of God.

Prophesying True to the Spirit of the Word

Though Israel had the scriptures, there were times when there was no law in place to address the need. In such cases, the prophets relied on God to speak to them in accordance with the spirit of the law. The "spirit" of the law was that which reflected God's character, nature, and will as expressed in the written law. For example, in 2 Kings 4:38-40, Elisha and the prophets being faced with death needed to hear from God. According to the story, someone unknowingly picked a poisonous plant to add to the stew. The result was contaminated food. There was and still is no law or scripture to provide guidance for dealing with this kind of situation. Therefore, Elisha looked to God for direction. Likewise, God answered him.

2 Corinthians 3:6 reads:

"The letter kills, but the Spirit gives life."

This verse establishes an idea. It establishes that there is a written law and a law of the Spirit. It teaches us that having the written word without the aid of the Holy Spirit is detrimental to us. We have many examples of this fact. Religions such as Jehovah Witnesses and Mormons are great examples. They both interpret scriptures without the guidance of the Holy Spirit. The result has been a new version of Christianity.

I once saw a nonbeliever on social media brilliantly articulate the scriptures. He could break down the Hebrew and Greek words. He could even elaborate on the culture of the times. From all appearances, he knew the scriptures. He knew the letter, but he did not know the Spirit of the scriptures. That being the case, he struggled with getting to the truth. It was fascinating to watch him talk about the scriptures, but never able to get the truth out of them. He did what most people do who try to understand the Bible without the Holy

Spirit; he leaned to his understanding and intellect. Likewise, everything he said sounded good. However, he could not provide a meaningful application for the information. It was all in his head. It reminded me of the number of sermons I have heard that were borne of the preacher's intellect. I can always tell when the brain is overly involved because our minds are limited in how we see the scriptures. One of the things that intrigue people about me is how I seamlessly tie the scriptures together and paint a clear picture of a concept. The only reason I can accomplish this impossible feat is that I allow the Holy Spirit to lead me into all truth. That does not mean that I irresponsibly throw out all sense of logic. After all, God gave me a brain for a reason. What it means, however, is that after I have studied the scriptures, I allow the Holy Spirit to bring it all together. When He does, everything is consistent. So, when I hear a sermon that I suspect to be a product of the intellect, I know it. I know it because it lacks biblical cohesiveness. Often while I am listening to a message, the Holy Spirit shows me errors in the sermon or teaching via what I call a virtual Bible. My virtual Bible is a Bible that appears to me in my mind. When I see it, God speaks to me about passages of scripture. He also brings it up when I am listening to sermons. Therefore, when the preacher says something wrong, the truth appears to me in scriptures. For instance, someone once said that God does not cause harm to people. As they were speaking about a dozen opposing views came to mind via scriptures.

What I want you to see is that there are times when we

need God to speak to us directly. Though the Bible is filled with practical wisdom, it does not address immediate needs. In such times, we need a word from God. For instance, who knew that the housing market would crash? Who knew that Texas would be hit by record-setting rain? Who knew that an earthquake would rock the entire eastern coast? Who knew that it would be so powerful that its effects would be felt as far as Canada? God knew all of this would happen. Because He knew, He also knew the best course of action to prepare for it. Furthermore, He would have freely told us how to prepare for all the aforementioned if we had asked.

We have great biblical examples of what happens when God speaks to us to address needs not covered in the scriptures. In Acts 11:27-30, the prophet Agabus prophesied a famine. Because of his prophecy, relief was sent to those affected. We can also see the power of God speaking in Genesis 41 when Pharaoh dreams of famine. It was the voice of God that allowed them to make provisions for that time. In fact, the miracle of the story was not the dream. It was the resulting knowledge. It was only because of God's voice that Joseph was able to craft a successful plan of action.

These depict situations that scripture does not directly address. The Bible tells us a lot about the future, but not every detail of it; hence, the examples presented. These stories validate the truth that God speaks when the scriptures are vague on an issue. That is not a criticism of the Bible. It is merely a reality. The scriptures are the framework of the believer's life. However, prophecy is God's way of filling in the gaps.

4
Chapter

The Divine Communication Hierarchy

Who Is Greatest?

In chapter one, I introduced the concept of a divine communication hierarchy. Now I want to delve deeper into that subject. Before we go any further, it is important that I encourage you to pay close attention to what I say in this chapter. Otherwise, you may misinterpret the point of this section.

As stated earlier, many saints believe in a hierarchy of divine communication. As an example, some of them believe that angels have higher communication value that prophets, leaders, and scripture. Therefore, they are often easily deceived by such experiences. The surreal nature of angelic encounters lends itself to a sense of authenticity and authority. Who wouldn't want to see angels? I have seen these majestic beings, and it is truly overwhelming. Yet, I must boldly state the unpopular: There is no hierarchy in God's communication system. In fact, at no point in the Bible does God encourage us to judge the validity of His words by our perceived ranking of the vessel through which it came. The only thing He instructs us to consider is the fruit of the message. With that said, I urge believers abandon the belief in a divine hierarchy of communication.

Let look at the subject further. Read these words captured by the prophet, Isaiah.

> *"For **My thoughts** are not your thoughts, nor are your ways My ways," says the Lord. "For as the heavens are higher than the earth, so are My ways higher than your ways, and **My thoughts** than your thoughts. "For as the rain comes down, and the snow from heaven, and do not return there, but water the earth, and make it bring forth and bud, that it may give seed to the sower and bread to the eater, So shall **My word** be that goes forth from My mouth; It shall not return to Me void, **but it shall accomplish** what I please, and it shall prosper in the thing for which I sent it." (Isaiah 55:8-11, NKJV)*

Pay close attention to the bolded parts of the text. Notice the progressive movement in the passage. It shifts from God's thoughts, *"My thoughts,"* to God's words, *"My word."* Then it moves from God's words to the materialization of those words, *"My word...shall accomplish what I sent it to do."* Here is the point: The Lord's words transition from intangible ideas to a substantive expression, to a concrete reality. There is a flow of continuity to the text. Thinking about this harmonious flow helps us see the relationship between the recorded and oratory voice of God. It reminds us that though they are different expressions, both are from the same source, using the same words, but in different ways. Furthermore, the passage does not present God's thoughts as better than His words. They are both valuable.

In the end, the passage captures two simple truths: God's word is embodied by the totality of an idea. The method or vehicle conveying that idea is irrelevant. An angel's message conveying God loves you is no more credible than the scriptures which tell you the same.

The second thing we learn is that God is consistent. The words in His mind aligns with what comes from His mouth. And what manifests, in reality, will also mirror His thoughts and words. In other words, every word from an angel, prophet, or scholar should echo the words Jesus declared regarding Himself. For example. Jesus tells us that He does not know the day or time of His return. Then how is it that people are duped every year by a charlatan announcing a specific date for Jesus's return? Here is a better illustration. How is it that some denounce the prophetic voice of God when Jesus declared that His sheep hear His voice? The inconsistency in both cases communicates that something is wrong. God is consistent!

Jonah's Incredible Example

I know that this idea is hard to grasp for some readers. Therefore, I am going to use a biblical illustration to show the consistent nature of God's voice. To do so, I am going to draw my example from a very familiar story—Jonah, the prophet on the run.

As most know, God told the prophet Jonah to go to Nineveh. His assignment was to deliver a judgement word against the city for its many atrocities. However, Jonah disobeyed God and boarded a ship heading in the opposite direction. His actions set in motion a series of divine events that holds keys to understanding the varied yet consistent nature of God's voice.

Look at Jonah 1:1. It reads:

*"Now **the word of the Lord came to Jonah** the son of Amittai, saying, 2 "Arise, go to Nineveh, that great city, and cry out against it; for their wickedness has come up before Me."'*

The phrase the "word of the Lord came to me, saying..." is interesting. We see this term used in multiple places in the Bible. For instance, the term is used all throughout the books of the prophets Ezekiel and Jeremiah. It is often interpreted by readers as God speaking audibly, though this assumption, is not verified in scripture. To understand the phrase, you must go to the book of Numbers chapter 12. In this chapter, God tells us how He speaks to prophets. He listed four ways in that passage: Dreams, visions, dark sayings, and a clear voice. The fourth, the voice is described by the Almighty as "rare." We can therefore, deduce that God spoke to Jonah in either a dream, vision, or dark saying.

Now look at verse 4, which reads:

*"But the Lord sent out a **great wind** on the sea, and there was a mighty tempest on the sea, so that the ship was about to be broken up."*

At this point, Jonah had charted a boat with some fellas. As recorded in verse four, God sent out a new message in the form of wind. It was such a strong wind that it violently threw the boat around on the sea. In fact, it was so tumultuous that the fishermen recognized it as a supernatural event. Then out of great fear they each called on their gods. While praying they noticed that the stranger, Jonah, did nothing. Then they questioned him about his unusually calm demeanor. Just then he confessed that he was the cause of their troubles. His words tell us that he understood exactly what God was saying through the storm. God used mother nature to convey the same thing he told Jonah in the dream: "Go to Nineveh, now!"

Verses 5-15 show us that Jonah's confession led to his demise. Upon acknowledging his error, he instructed the men to sacrifice him to the sea. So, that is what they did. Then something else supernatural happened. A huge fish, prepared by God's hands, swallowed the man of God.

Look at verse 17. It reads:

*"Now the Lord **had prepared a great fish to swallow Jonah**. And Jonah was in the belly of the fish three days and three nights."*

Once in the belly of the fish, chapter two records his prayer of repentance to God. This time we see God's voice manifested in the circumstances. He was still saying the same thing through the circumstances that He said in the dream, and by the storm. Jonah's prayer was evidence that he recognized that God orchestrated his unusual circumstances. In fact, upon repenting, the Bible tells us that the fish spat the prophet out of its mouth onto the shoreline.

Next, let's read chapter 3:1. It reads:

"Now the word of the Lord came to Jonah the second time, saying, "Arise, go to Nineveh, that great city, and preach to it the message that I tell you.""

This is now the fourth time God spoke to Jonah. Each time, through different mediums, He said the same thing, "Go to Nineveh, Now!" Are you seeing it yet?

The Second Time Around

Here is a second example found in the latter half of Jonah's incredible journey. The after discussion between God and his prophet shows us more of the same pattern.

As the story goes, God relented from destroying the city of Nineveh because they repented of their deeds. God's decision to withhold harm infuriated the prophet. Understanding the historical background of Nineveh, and considering the ordeal he endured to get to that point, I can identify with his displeasure. Still, our God is merciful, and Jonah knew that.

The Divine Communication Hierarchy

Our second example starts in chapter four. Overwhelmed by his anger, Jonah lashed out at God in prayer. Then God responded to his anger with a question in chapter 4:4, He asked him, *"Is it right for you to be angry?"* Jonah answered, *"Yes!"* Then he left the city and sat on a hill, hoping that God would change His mind and destroy the city. While there, God caused a plant to grow to protect him from the sun. Then He prepared a worm to eat the plant. This action caused the east wind to blow the sun's heat in Jonah's direction. Of course, this further angered the already irritated man of God. Finally, on the heels of this illustration, God asked him again about his anger. This time, He even went as far as using the plant and worm as an illustration with the sole purpose of reasoning with the prophet.

Here is what I want you to see in this scenario; God spoke to him three times in this part of the story. Once in an audible voice. We know this because the man of God is awake and praying. The second time God spoke, He used a plant, worm, wind, heat, and the sun. These equate to God displaying His voice through nature and circumstances. Lastly, God spoke the last time in a voice the prophet heard. Notice that the manifestations, though different, are all God's voice.

We see a similar pattern in the first part of Jonah's story. God used multiple expressions to say the same thing. The first time the word was "Go to Nineveh, Now!" The second time He said, "Why are you mad?" Though God used multiple methods to communicate His thoughts, the message was consistent. Also, take note to the fact that the prophet does

47

not regard one method more than the others. In other words, God's voice in the circumstances were just as valuable as the voice he heard with his ears.

When teaching on the subject of hearing the voice of God, it is important to do so correctly. When taught and executed properly, believers experience the voice of God in a seamless manner. There is absolutely no reason to fear that prophecy will devalue the scriptures. If the prophetic word is really from God, it will enhance and establish it, instead of competing with its place in the Christian's heart.

The Danger of Ranking the Voice of God

Ranking the voice of God can be hazardous to the believer. You may not readily see the danger in this behavior, but it is present. We even have a few examples of this harmful practice in the scriptures. 1 Kings 13:11-25 presents a story of a prophet that God killed for not fully following His instructions. The story also reveals the mindset that delivered this poor guy to death's door.

The story began when God told the young prophet to go into the city and declare an unfavorable message to the king. With His initial instructions He also told this man that he was not to leave the city through the same gates he entered it. Finally, God told him not to stop and eat or drink anything in the city. The story goes on to show us that the man comprehended God's instructions, but later disobeyed them. His disobedience led to his unfortunate death.

How do we know that the prophet understood God's com-

The Divine Communication Hierarchy

mand? And why did he disobey Him? Let's start with the first question. We know that he understood God's instructions because he refused two invitations to dinner. The first invitation came by way of the king. After the prophet delivered the harsh word of the Lord, the humbled king wanted to make amends. But the prophet, in obedience to God, refused the offer. This bit of information confirms that the prophet clearly understood God's instructions regarding food and drink.

The second invitation came from an older prophet as he attempted to leave the city. The older prophet, informed by his students, of the young prophet's supernatural exploits, desperately desired to bring the man back to his home. So he invited him to dinner. But, again, with God's instructions present in his mind, the young man rejected the offer. Again, this demonstrates his comprehension of God's instructions. Then the unthinkable happened. The older prophet, lied and told the younger prophet that an angel spoke to him requesting that he bring the young man back to his house. So, the young prophet submitted himself to the older prophet's words.

Some people use this story to teach about the dangers of intimidation. Their focus is on the fact that the older man used his influence to persuade the younger man. I agree that a hint of that element exists in the story. But here's my perspective on the text. It is evident that the only reason the older man was able to manipulate the younger one was due to the young prophet's belief in a hierarchy of divine communication.

Here is the justification for my statement. First, he rejected the older prophet's initial offer. That means that he was not too enamored with the older man. While he may have used some intimidation tactics, they did not affect the man's decision. Second, the young man only changed his mind after the older prophet told him that an angel changed God's marching orders.

Verses 20-25 show us the consequences of this type of thinking. So many believers shipwreck their lives because of this very same philosophy. God told them to go left, then some divine encounter said otherwise. Then they find themselves trap in a hopeless mess. Just consider the countless stories of those who gave away their life savings because a popular preacher attached a promise of wealth to instructions to sow a financial seed. How many divorces are the result of following a dream to marry someone who is not a believer? How many spouses have left their husband or wife because of a prophetic word that contradicted the scriptures? Five thousand people lost their lives to Jim Jones because they regarded his revelation over the advice of real men and women of God. What makes us submit our lives to such grave decisions? We do so because we exalt one of God's communicative expressions above the rest.

If It's in the Bible, It Must be True

I think I made it clear that I have the highest regard for the Bible. It is the voice of God that governs my life. Yet, how do you respect it and disagree with those sharing its truth out of context? The espousing of ideas rooted in misinterpreted scriptures happens all of the time. For example, Jehovah's Witnesses canvas neighborhoods frequently making converts. Their greatest weapon, even against Christians, is the Bible. They are often skilled in maneuvering around it and using their version of the truth to beat you into seeing their point of view. In fact, these types of cultish groups know how to corner believers into listening to them by simply using the logic, "If it is in the bible, it must be true." They know that we regard it highly, therefore, it is easy to convince the immature among us that someone taught us wrongly.

In the fall of 2019, my twin brother and I decided to go out to lunch together. On our way, we saw two fellas standing on the curb, sharing their faith. As we passed by, they attempted to stop us, but we waved them off. We were hungry and, on a schedule, and we did not have time to stop and talk. On our way back from lunch, we saw them again. And, again, they attempted to get our attention, so this time we gave them an opportunity to make their presentation. One of the guys kept reaching out to those who passed by, while the other attended to us. He told us that Jesus was coming back soon, and we needed to be ready. The term "be ready" was a ploy to get us to come to his church for bible study. We kindly declined his offer and told him were already believers in Christ. For whatever reason, that was not a good enough answer. Then he began to warn us that Jesus was coming back and his church was the only one in the world teaching the truth. I told him that was not possible. Then he went for a kill move. He said,

"Let me show it to you in the Bible. If you are a believer, then you will respect the word of God." I told him, "No. I have all respect for the word of God, but I know that whatever you are going to say is going to be erroneous." Then I told him that I don't have time to engage in a back and forth about the scriptures." He then got a bit agitated and insisted that my brother and I let him show us his teaching. Finally, I said this to him, "The Bible says that God gives his secrets to His servants, plural, the prophets, plural. How is it then that your church has the only revelation of the end of days and Jesus' return?" Then we walked off and told him to have a good day.

These guys were part of a cult. It was my second confrontation with them. My brother and I evaded their deception. Still, it makes you wonder; how many people did not survive their encounter with these guys? How many people joined this cult? The better question is, how did I survive my face-off with this cult twice? How was I able to disarm their attempts to use the Bible as an authority to beat me into accepting their false beliefs? Well, it is simple. I do not adhere to a hierarchy of divine communication. Instead, I hold fast to the idea that God's truth is parallel. I also view the Bible as "an" authority not "the" authority in my life. I know that is a super-risky statement. Just keep reading, and it will all make sense. What do I mean by my statement? How can I value God's words and not allow the Bible to be the only authority in my life? Simple, the Bible itself tells us that there are three that agree in heaven; the Father, the Word, and the Holy Spirit (See 1 John 5:7).

The Three Must Agree

Here is something to think about: If every faction of Christianity bases their religious beliefs on the same Bible, who has the right interpretation of it? Are all believers supposed to speak in tongues or not? Are we saved once, or is it a process that requires us to stay the course throughout our lifetime? These are all questions plaguing the Church today. How can we better ensure that we commit ourselves to following the right interpretation of truth?

As mentioned previously, 1 John 5:7 tells us how to do it. It tells us that the Spirit of God's voice counts as much as the voice of the Word. Going back to the beginning of the chapter, this is again, a depiction of the consistent nature of God. In relationship to 1 John 5:7, the word consistent means that the words in the Father's mouth are the same as the ones read in the Word and heard via the Spirit.

In both of my encounters with this cult, I felt the Spirit of God warring against the scriptures put forth by these people. I knew that something was wrong when God seemed to be at war with Himself. Please do not misunderstand me. I am a long-time Christian. As such, I know that some will use my statement as a crutch anytime the scriptures challenge their behavior. That is not my point. I am not talking about the justification of our arrogance. I am referring to being connected to God in such a way that we know when the Word and Spirit are working together, and when they are not.

Just consider Jesus' example in Luke 4. There He was when some spirit used the scriptures to suggest that He throw

Himself off of a temple. Jesus did not concur with the words just because they were in the divine text. Instead, He realized that the spirit behind the words was not operating in agreement with the Spirit of the word.

Co-Equal, Not Co-Responsible

We know that the Trinity consist of the Father, Son, and Holy Spirit. Most of the Church accepts the belief that they are co-equal in every way. They share the same remarkable qualities of omnipresence, omnipotence, and omniscience; they are everywhere at the same time, all-powerful, and all-knowing. They are alike in every way except one; they don't have the same responsibilities? Did you know that within the Godhead there is structure and order? Look at what Jesus told His disciples;

> *However, when He, the Spirit of truth, has come, He will guide you into all truth; for He will not speak on His own authority, but whatever He hears He will speak; and He will tell you things to come. (John 16:13, NKJV)*

Also, look at what Jesus said about God the Father.

> *"Then Jesus answered and said to them, "Most assuredly, I say to you, the Son can do nothing of Himself, but what He sees the Father do; for whatever He does, the Son also does in like manner." (John 5:19)*

The Divine Communication Hierarchy

Look at 1 Corinthians 12:4-6:

"There are diversities of gifts, but the same Spirit. There are differences of ministries, but the same Lord. And there are diversities of activities, but it is the same God who works all in all."

All three passages teach us that God has structure and order within Himself. That idea is both complex and impressive at the same time. It also conveys that it is possible to be equal but different. It shows us that the Trinity shares the throne, but their responsibilities are unique.

One thing that offends people about the prophetic is the unfounded insinuation that prophecy is elevated above the scriptures. Somehow people assume that the Spirit of the Word is greater or lesser than the Word itself. Neither is true. The Spirit of the Word is not greater or less than the Word. They are co-equal in authority, but their purposes, while aligned with each other, are fundamentally different.

Let's look at the interesting dichotomy in 1 John 5:7 and John 16:13. One tells us that the three persons in the Godhead agree, while the other indicates that the Spirit will not speak on His own "authority." Authority is an important word. The Spirit of God does not have lesser authority than Jesus and the Father. Yet, He willingly chooses to play a specific role. The passage is clear that He has independent authority, hence the term "His authority." It is equally clear that He chooses to submit to the greater will of the Trinity, called God.

When we think about the prophetic word and the written word in terms of their roles, we are less confused by their ability to co-exist. For instance, Paul tells Timothy that the scriptures are suitable for developing the saints and the man or woman of God (2 Tim. 3:16-17). The written word of God has the purpose of creating boundaries and developing our lives. The prophetic word, however, is for direction, vision, and finetuning the believer. Reversing their roles can lead to chaos, confusion, frustration, and even death.

For example, my mother developed cancer when she was 57 years old. By 58 years old, she was dead. During that year, she decided to forgo traditional cancer treatment and opted for natural herbal methodology. As she did, she found scriptures regarding healing and placed her faith in God's written word. After a long time of not seeing any evidence of change, I asked her this question; "Ma, did you hear from God yet? She said, "No." Then I wondered why she disregarded the doctor's counsel to pursue an alternative method of treatment. She had also been reading a book by a guy opposed to chemotherapy. In his book, he gave all kinds of advice against it and recommended the alternatives my mother used. Being curious, I read a few pages. As I did, I noticed that this man included no personal references to surviving a cancer ordeal. So, I turned to my mother and asked another question. I asked. "Ma, did this guy go through cancer? She replied, "No!" To which I said, "Then why are you listening to him. He has not tested his own theories?" Only a few short months later, she passed away.

The Divine Communication Hierarchy

She was standing on the Word, the development tool, for guidance. What she really needed at that moment was the Spirit, God's guidance tool. When we get the roles out of whack, we fall short every time. I have witnessed many stories like my mother's. Most of them concluded in disappointment. For my mom, it resulted in death; for others, it was financial, emotional, or mental ruin. That is why I am writing this book. As stated before, my intention is not to downplay the word while playing up the Spirit. My goal is to get you to understand the need for both. We need the Word. That is a fact. Still, we also need to be able to hear and respond to what the Spirit is saying to the Church. If we choose one over the other, we run the risk of error.

We can never allow a prophetic word to rule our lives when it contradicts or competes with the written word of God. Likewise, we cannot let our understanding of the scriptures guide us in opposition to the Spirit of God. They are not competing for a first-place prize. They are both first.

Let me give you one more scripture that illustrates the harmony of the Word and the Spirit.

"But the Helper, the Holy Spirit, whom the Father will send in My name, He will teach you all things, and bring to your remembrance all things that I said to you." (John 14:26, NKJV)

Look at the harmony at work in the passage. The Word is prophesying about the Spirit's arrival, purpose, and operation. In doing so, the Word informs us that the Spirit will bring to our memory the things the Word said to us. What an incredible depiction of the unity in the Trinity. Finally, we need to recognize that the three are required to have agreement. We all embrace the voice and authority of the Father and the Word. Now we need to welcome the voice of the Holy Spirit. We will find that easy to do once we abandon the idea of divine hierarchy.

5
―― Chapter ――

Common Arguments Against Hearing God's Voice

It would be folly on my part if I did not to consider the argument of those opposed to hearing God's voice. Therefore, I am going to tackle the most common misunderstandings about prophetic expression.

God spoke by Jesus, the last prophet

The idea that Jesus was the last prophet is preposterous. Some argue this idea based on Hebrews 1:1. We read it in an earlier chapter, but let's look at this verse again. It reads:

> "God who in various ways, spoke to us by the prophets has in these last days chosen to speak by His Son, Jesus Christ."

I have learned a few things about biblical study over the years. Learning how to be neutral in my approach to the scriptures was an important lesson. I find that those who examine the scriptures with a predetermined point of view often misinterpret them. Likewise, I believe that those who see this passage as a way of excluding prophecy from today's church taint the real meaning of this text. Why am I making such an inflammatory statement? Well, let's examine this passage in light of the facts as viewed through the whole body of scripture.

Let's start with Ephesians 4:11. It reads:

"And He Himself gave some to be apostles, some prophets, some evangelists, and some pastors and teachers,"

Here we clearly see that Jesus appointed prophets. How is it that Jesus was the last prophet if He appointed prophets? If you read the whole body of text, you see that these gifts were given after His ascension (See Eph. 11:7-10). Based on the passage, it is highly unlikely that Jesus thought of Himself as the last prophet.

Some people take it a bit further and assert that there are no examples of New Testament prophets. This is another odd belief. It does not take a biblical scholar to see the error in this idea. The biblical record provides an overwhelming amount of evidence to the contrary.

Looking again at Ephesians 4:11, we see the truth in plain

sight. Again, it establishes the fact that this gift continues into the New Testament era. Not only that, but we have many biblical accounts of New Testament prophets. For example, Acts 15:32 calls Judas and Silas prophets. Acts 21:10 speaks of a prophet named Agabus. Acts 21:9 recalls that Phillip had four virgin daughters who prophesied. Lastly, we have 1 Corinthians 14:29-32, which clearly states that there were prophets. It even goes a step further and establishes a protocol for prophetic ministry.

Where does the idea that Jesus was the last prophet originate? As mentioned, many use Hebrews 1:1. In conjunction with that verse, others rely on the "silent period" theory. The concept of the silent period says that there were no prophets after Malachi until Jesus. It is believed that God was quiet during those years. It is also widely accepted that He did not speak again until Jesus arrived in the earth; hence, the many who misinterpret Hebrews 1:1.

However, please note again, that to believe such requires us to ignore the obvious. Firstly, to think such you must to minimize the ministry of John the Baptist. Jesus was very clear that John was a prophet. Let's look at what Jesus said about John in Luke 7:28.

> *"For I say to you, among those born of women, there is not a greater prophet than John the Baptist; but he who is least in the kingdom of God is greater than he.""*

Is God Still Speaking?

We also have other great examples of people hearing from God during the "silent period." There was Mary, the mother of Jesus. She received word about her pregnancy from an angel (Luke 1:26-38). God spoke to Elizabeth's husband, Zechariah, about their son, John the Baptist (Luke 1:5-22). Then there was a man named Simeon who was in the temple whose sole purpose in living was to see the Christ. Let's look at this one.

> "Now there was a man in Jerusalem called Simeon, who was righteous and devout. He was waiting for the consolation of Israel, and the Holy Spirit was on him. **It had been revealed to him by the Holy Spirit** that he would not die before he had seen the Lord's Messiah. Moved by the Spirit, he went into the temple courts. When the parents brought in the child Jesus to do for him what the custom of the Law required, Simeon took him in his arms and praised God, saying: "Sovereign Lord, as you have promised, you may now dismiss your servant in peace. For my eyes have seen your salvation, which you have prepared in the sight of all nations: a light for revelation to the Gentiles, and the glory of your people Israel." The child's father and mother marveled at what was said about him. Then Simeon blessed them and said to Mary, his mother: "This child is destined to cause the falling and rising of many in Israel, and to be a sign that will be spoken against, so that the thoughts of many hearts will be revealed. And a sword will pierce your own soul too.""

Then, we read of a woman prophetess named Anna the prophetess. While in the temple, God spoke to her about the coming Christ (See Luke 2:36-38.). As you can see, God was speaking during the so-called silent period.

Finally, as we consider that Jesus was not the last prophet, we must discuss Revelation chapter 11. This chapter speaks of two prophets that will arise in the last days. This really brings to light the fallacy of this idea. How is it that Jesus was the last prophet if He intends to send forth prophets in the last days?

As you can see, this argument is inconsistent with the scriptures. Jesus was definitely not the last prophet.

Anything we hear from God rises to the level of scripture and adds to the biblical record

In an earlier chapter, I detailed the different types of words that God speaks to us. They were words that foretell, advise, inform, direct, judge, warn, correct, and bless. Each type of word reveals to us that God spoke with one of these purposes in mind. At no point, other than when God provided Moses the law, did God ever speak to create scripture. God spoke to people who needed to hear from Him. Furthermore, for our benefit, those words were recorded, regarded as valuable, and canonized. Nevertheless, they were not spoken with the intent of providing us the scriptures.

I'm not exactly sure how we even came to that conclusion. Again, no place in the Bible supports this idea. Most people holding to this rationale believe that I Timothy is the foundation for this idea. We read it earlier, but let's look at it again. It reads:

> "All scripture is given by inspiration of God, and is profitable for doctrine, for reproof, for correction, and for instruction in righteousness."

If we are to exegete this scripture properly, then we must examine a few things. First, it does not say that the scripture is doctrine. It says that scripture is good for doctrine; Big difference! We have somehow concluded that scriptures are doctrine. In so doing we equate what was written as things God said. However, if you objectively look at the scriptures, you discover that not all things written in the Bible are from God's mouth. Instead, they are records of various stories that include things God said to biblical characters.

For instance, most of the book of Job records discussions between Job and his friends. The least amount of discussion in the book of Job comes from God. Then something interesting happens at the end of the book of Job. Verse 42:7 says:

> "And so it was, after the LORD had spoken these words to Job, that the LORD said to Eliphaz the Temanite, "My wrath is aroused against you and your two friends, **for you have not spoken of Me what is right**, as My servant Job has.

Notice that God condemned the words spoken by Job's friends. How many sermons have been devised from the words spoken by these men? How about this one? Job 22:28 reads:

"You will also declare a thing. And it will be established for you: So light will shine upon thy ways."

How many times have you heard this preached? Did you know that it is a statement from one of Job's friends? Did you know that it was spoken in a spirit of accusation against Job's character? We have invented an entire doctrine about "decree and declare," and it is based on something that God Himself declared not right!

This example makes a case for why we should not consider everything written in the Bible to be God's words. Yes, the Bible contains God's words, but not everything in it is what God said or agrees with.

I know that is a risky statement. I also know that many will take it out of its context to make it fit a nefarious narrative. Nevertheless, I have already established the essential need and value of the Bible in the believer's life. Furthermore, I have used nothing but the Bible to establish my argument. Finally, my statement is not without merit. There are plenty of examples that support the idea that the Bible records God's words, though not everything in it is from His mouth.

Here is an excellent example. In Luke 4:1-11, Satan attempts to lure Jesus into sin. To do so, he quotes the scriptures. It is evident that though Satan used the word of God, those words were not coming from God's mouth. They were not even used in the right context. To combat this satanic assault, Jesus also quotes the scriptures.

We see this kind of out-of-context preaching often, don't we? How often have you heard someone quote scripture to justify their actions? In their minds, the words are from God, though they are not used in the right way. Hopefully, the point is clear.

Some of you might say, "Sir, this is more of an example of twisting God's words." Therefore, let's look at a more obvious example.

I Kings 13 records a story of a prophet whom God killed for his disobedience. The story starts with an incredible prophetic display from a budding prophet. God told him to deliver the prophetic word. He also forbade him from exiting the city by the same entrance. He was further instructed not to eat or drink in the place where the prophecy was delivered. After withstanding an invitation from the king to disobey God, he encountered an older prophet. These are the words of the senior prophet to the younger prophet recorded in verse 18:

> *He said to him, "I too am a prophet as you are, and an angel spoke to me by the word of the LORD, saying, 'Bring him back with you to your house, that he may eat bread and drink water." (He was lying to him.)*

It does not get any plainer than this. Note that the words in parenthesis are a part of the verse. It is clear that these words "in the Bible" are not God's words. In fact, the same prophet that lied to him prophesied the young man's death. Let's read the passage that shows us God's words. Verse 20-22 read:

> Now it happened, as they sat at the table, that the word of the LORD came to the prophet who had brought him back; and he cried out to the man of God who came from Judah, saying, "Thus says the LORD: 'Because you have disobeyed the word of the LORD, and have not kept the commandment which the LORD your God commanded you, but you came back, ate bread, and drank water in the place of which the LORD said to you, "Eat no bread and drink no water," your corpse shall not come to the tomb of your fathers.' "

It is interesting, isn't it? Can you see now that not everything in the Bible is God's word, though the Bible encompasses God's word? Though the body of work is God-inspired, it does not mean that every word is holy. For that reason, the apostle Paul encourages young Pastor Timothy to rightly divide the word of truth. Not doing so, easily leads to preaching, from the scriptures, ideas that the scriptures do not support. Worst, it could lead to participating in dangerous practices forbidden by the scriptures.

The Word of the Lord Verses the Word of God

To better understand my position on the matter, we must answer a question. Is there a difference between "the word of God" and "the word of the LORD?" This may surprise you, but there is a difference between the two. The differences are subtle, yet, it is important to establish the uniqueness of both terms. People opposed to the idea of the Bible and prophecy co-existing believe that everything God said and says rises to the level of the scriptures. In other words, they believe that the word of the LORD becomes the word of God. However, this is not true. As we move forward, I will show you why it is neither biblical nor sensible.

Let's start by defining why it is unbiblical to believe that everything God says becomes scripture. Most believers refer to the Bible by the term "the word of God." They do so because scripture uses the term many times. For instance, Paul unveils the concept of the armor of God in Ephesians 6:17. As he does, he compels us to ensure that we have the sword of the Spirit which he says is "the word of God." In turn, we infer that Paul's reference to the word of God means, the scriptures. Furthermore, we have every right to accept this as truth. We even have a great example in Luke 4:1-14 of Jesus using the word as a weapon. When faced with temptation in the passage, He used the scriptures to fight off the devil's temptations. His example pairs well with the idea in Ephesians 6.

We also have a great example in Psalm 119:105. David says, *"Your word is a lamp unto my feet and a light unto my path."* It is clear from the context and the surrounding verses, that David's use of the word "word" refers to the law, otherwise called the scriptures in 1 Timothy 3:16.

However, there is another term that we often confuse with "the word of God." It is the term "the word of the Lord." What is the word of the Lord? Where do we find examples of it in scripture? The term is actually used in several places in the scriptures.

Let's look at a few:

- *But the word of the Lord came to me saying, "You have shed much blood and have made great wars; you shall not build a house for My name, because you have shed much blood on the earth in My sight (1 Chron. 22:8, NKJV)*

- *Then the word of the LORD came to me, saying: (Jer. 1:4, NKJV)*

- *Moreover, the word of the LORD came to me, saying, "Jeremiah, what do you see?" And I said, "I see the branch of an almond tree." (Jer. 1:11, NKJV)*

(You will find more examples all throughout the book of Jeremiah and the prophets Ezekiel and Zechariah. Note that each use of the term refers to ongoing words from the mouth of God.)

The term "*word of the LORD*", as we see it in our examples, describes forthcoming words from God's mouth. It differs from the word of God. One term expresses what God has said, while the other depicts what He is saying. When referencing the sword of the Spirit in Ephesians 6, it is easy to conclude that the passage refers to the scriptures—what God has said. Again, Jesus' example furthers that assumption. However, the passage makes no clear distinction regarding which term Paul is referring to. I think I know why.

Paul, like most of us who believe God is actively speaking, makes no distinction between what God said and is saying. He understood and valued the reality that the scriptures, as well as prophecy, are both valuable and powerful mediums of God's voice. How can I make such a statement? Well, just consider that Jesus used the scriptures as His sword to fend off the devil in Luke 4. Yet, Paul tells Timothy to use the prophecies spoken over his life to fend off discouragement. Both Jesus and Timothy were at war. Likewise, both of them had access to the same scriptures. Yet, one used the word of God to defend Himself, while the other used the word of the LORD.

It is really important to understand the difference between these two terms. If not properly understood, it is easy to make the assertion that all of the words from God's mouth become scripture. Please know that every word of the LORD does not rise to the level of the word of God. Later, in the next section, I further clarify the matter.

Now let's look at what makes this belief senseless. Let's start by looking at some of the things God said to various people. First, let's start by examining Genesis 21. In this passage of scripture, Abraham kicks Hagar and Ishmael out of his life. He does so because Sarah witnesses Ishmael harassing Isaac.

This spawned feelings of jealousy in Sarah's heart and she told Abraham that Hagar and her son had to leave. This was problematic for Abraham. Ishmael was also his son. Being emotionally torn about the situation, he pondered about what to do. While he did, God spoke to him. What He said was recorded as part of the divine record we call the scriptures. The words that God spoke to Abraham have no personal significance to us. We cannot apply these words to our life. They are merely historical information that give us the proper context for understanding our faith. The words themselves are not scripture but part of scripture.

As the story progresses, Abraham evicts Hagar and her child from his home. As the two desperate and brokenhearted souls travel alone, the son becomes dehydrated. Not being able to withstand watching her son die, she puts him under a shrub. While weeping, God hears the child crying and speaks to Hagar. Look at what He said. (Gen. 21:17-18)

> *And God heard the voice of the lad. Then the angel of God called to Hagar out of heaven, and said to her, "What ails you, Hagar? Fear not, for God has heard the voice of the lad where he is. Arise, lift up the lad and hold him with your hand, for I will make him a great nation."*

Again, we see a great example of words from God that are part of the biblical record, but not scripture by nature. We cannot take God's word's to Hagar and apply them to our life. Neither were they spoken with that intent in mind. In fact,

Moses is the one retelling this story. She did not even think enough of these words to write them down. Less this confuses you, let's look at a contrasting example.

In Exodus 31:18, God speaks to Moses. When He does, he provides Moses a written set of instructions that we refer to as the Ten Commandments. Later on, God speaks to him several more times. Each time Moses captures those words in what is called the Book of the Law. There is one key factor in Moses' experience to note; He was instructed by God to write down words that governed peoples' lives. Whereas, Hagar's words were merely God's intervention in a hurting single parent's life. Her words, while important historically, have no relevance today. I would also assert that her words, though recorded in scripture are not themselves scripture. There are many examples in the Bible of words from God like those of Hagar's.

The next example comes from 2 Kings 7:1-2. It reads:

Then Elisha said, "Hear the word of the Lord. Thus says the Lord: 'Tomorrow about this time a seah of fine flour shall be sold for a shekel, and two seahs of barley for a shekel, at the gate of Samaria.'" So an officer on whose hand the king leaned answered the man of God and said, "Look, if the Lord would make windows in heaven, could this thing be?" And he said, "In fact, you shall see it with your eyes, but you shall not eat of it."

Again, we see that God's words, though important historically, are not applicable to us. They are recorded as reference in the scripture. They are not like Moses' words. This story can also be contrasted against Habakkuk.

In Habakkuk 2:2 the prophet is instructed to "write" the vision *(prophetic word)* of God. Jeremiah is also instructed to write down his words in Jeremiah 36:2. It reads:

"Take a scroll of a book and write on it all the words that I have spoken to you against Israel, against Judah, and against all the nations, from the days that I spoke to you, from the days of Josiah even to this day."

The next verse tells us why God wanted the prophets to record His words. It reads:

"It may be that the house of Judah will hear all the adversities which I purpose to bring upon them, that everyone may turn from his evil way, that I may forgive their iniquity and their sin."

Look at the difference between the scenarios in 2 Kings and Habakkuk and Jeremiah. All three contain words from God. Yet, God only wants Habakkuk's and Jeremiah's words recorded. The two prophet's words later become part of the highly regarded Books of the Prophets. God obviously wanted those words to be scripture.

Now let's look at something else. These examples beg us to

ask a question. Why didn't God require Elisha to record any of his prophetic words? After all, he and his predecessor, Elijah, are highly esteemed in scripture. Elijah, in fact, has become somewhat of a legend within Christianity. We know that these two guys spoke on God's behalf. Yet, we have no record of their words from God, other than what we read in someone else's account. Neither has a prophetic book included in the Book of the Prophets. They are not alone. We have many examples in the Bible of prophets who spoke God's words that were not regarded as scripture. This is true in both the Old and New Testaments.

If all words from God rise to the level of scripture, where are the words that God spoke to these lost voices? Where are the scriptures and books produced by their encounters with God? Acts 21:9 says that the evangelist Philip had four virgin daughters that prophesied. Where are their prophecies? 2 Kings 2 reveals several schools of prophets. Where are their words? In 1 Corinthians 14:26-33 Paul teaches believers the proper protocol for allowing prophecy to operate in the service. That means that the Corinthians actively heard and relayed messages from God. Where are their revelations?

Are you starting to see how unbiblical and senseless it is to believe that everything God says should be regarded as scripture? I certainly hope so.

The next section goes into further detail on the matter. I will make plain the reality that God spoke to mankind many times, and each time with a clear purpose. Creating scripture was merely one of His many purposes for speaking to to us.

Three Stages of Revelation

Here is another reason we should not believe that God spoke with the intent of giving us scriptures. The Bible reveals three stages of revelation from God. There is revelation that is foundational, framing *(building)*, and personal. Each of these stages appears in the scriptures, and each one tells us something about the nature of God's communication.

Foundational Revelation

The term foundational means exactly what it says. Foundational revelation is that which establishes the basis for the kingdom of God. They are the guiding principles upon which we build other ideas are built. There are only four people in the scriptures with such revelation. There was Adam, Abraham, Moses, and Jesus. These men were granted information from God that set the course for their generations.

Cornerstone Words

To really understand foundational revelation, you must understand the cornerstone principle. In the world of construction, the cornerstone is the very first stone laid in the foundation of a building. It is imperative that the stone is laid correctly because it determines the strength and accuracy of every stone that follows. If it is laid crooked, the whole foundation is misaligned. Even worse, it can lead to structural damage, as the edges of the walls built upon it won't come together correctly. As you can see, the cornerstone is fundamental to the success of the building.

The same is true of God's kingdom. Jesus is referred to as a cornerstone. Also, God tells us in Isaiah that He is a builder adding precept upon precept and line upon line. That being the case, God has built His kingdom the same way. To do so, He selected special people to unveil information that determines the direction of His people. The first stone was laid in the Garden Eden. He told Adam that there was a Seed that would come to resolve the sin issue. That is the first time the Bible mentions Jesus, and it sets the tone for everything else that follows. The Bible says there is no other foundation that we can build on other than Christ (See 1 Cor. 3:11).

The next foundational stone was laid in the life of Abraham. Abraham received insight from God that established the premise for the existence of the nation of Israel. Those principles prevail in that nation until this day.

The next person to receive this level of revelation was Moses. Again, we see in the book of Exodus that God gave Moses insight that governed the entire nation. It was through Moses that they learned how to dress, eat, worship, work, interact with each other, deal with other nations, and more. Moses' revelation was critical to the formation of a people.

The last example of this type of insight comes from Jesus. It was through Abraham that God created a people for Himself. And through Moses He created Judaism. However, it was through Jesus that God created Christianity. It is so important to understand what I am unveiling. Though all of these men, Adam, Abraham, and Moses, built on each other, they ultimately built on Christ. Certain persecutors of the

Christian faith always ask the dumb question, "Was Jesus a Christian?" The question is meant to make Christians doubt their faith by asserting that we call ourselves by something our leader didn't. I know that it sounds stupid. Actually, it is very idiotic. It's stupid because we call ourselves Christians because we follow the ways of Christ, who is Jesus. Our name reflects our commitment to His teachings. Understanding this truth is foundational to our faith and embracing Jesus as the Christ allows us to successfully build on the direction that He set for His belief system. Moreover, the cornerstone is the revelation of Jesus as the Christ.

Now, it is essential to understand that there will never again be a person of this caliber. No one will ever be able to hear from God on the level of these people. For that reason, Hebrews tells us that God spoke in various ways to the prophets, but has this last time spoken by His Son. In other words, God is not going to lay another foundational stone.

It is crucial to embrace this truth. Every person that has attempted to hear from God on this level has redefined Jesus. Efforts to redefine the person of Jesus always leads to the creation of alternative forms of Christianity. The Mormon religion is a perfect example of this truth. Joseph Smith created Mormonism after an angel appeared to him and told that there was more to know about Jesus. He then added to the foundation, thereby creating another book. That book is supposed to contain more foundational revelation. This is where we step into dangerous waters. It is also what creates a well-founded fear in those opposed to the idea of God speaking today. Many legitimately fear that someone will do just as Joseph Smith, thereby moving into error. Likewise, we have seen it happen with the invention of the Gospel of Inclusion. This doctrine attempts to redefine the foundational truths of our faith. The thing that makes this doctrine so wrong is that it skews our understanding of God's nature—defining who God is at the core of foundational revelation.

New Age is an erroneous foundational doctrine. So is as Islam, Confucianism, Hinduism, and the rest. All of these try to explain the essence of God. Each has a point of view regarding His character. They are foundational in nature and are man's efforts to set the course for our understanding of God. Jesus defined God for us, and no one will ever have that level of revelation again. He was and is the final revelation on the nature and character of God.

Framing Revelation

The understanding that Jesus is the final foundational revelation of God leads us to the next type of revelation, framing revelation. I also call this building revelation. What is framing revelation? Remember our passage in Isaiah 28:9-11, regarding how God builds His kingdom. Let's look at it. It reads:

> *"Whom will he teach knowledge? And whom will he make to understand the message? Those just weaned from milk? Those just drawn from the breasts? For precept must be upon precept, precept upon precept, Line upon line, line upon line, Here a little, there a little."*

For with stammering lips and another tongue He will speak to this people,

Look at what God says about the way He doles out knowledge. He says revelation is given to us a little at a time and in a systematic way. That means that no one gets it all at once. It teaches us that God's truth is progressive. That is important because God is still building on the foundation that He set. However, He warns us, via Jesus, to be careful about how we build. He cautions us in His parable that building on the wrong foundation can lead to ruin (See Matt. 7:24-27). That means that we are only safe if we build on His revelation of who God character.

Here is the revelatory principle in Jesus's parable; we (believers) build on everything He said and says. That means that there are foundational truths. It further means that with that foundation are other ideas needed to finalize the structure. It is another way of God showing us "line upon line, precept upon precept..."

Let's look at Paul's words in 1 Corinthians 11:10-11.

According to the grace of God which was given to me, as a wise master builder I have laid the foundation, and another builds on it. But let each one take heed how he builds on it. For no other foundation can anyone lay than that which is laid, which is Jesus Christ.

Paul also says that he laid a foundation. What is the foundation? He names the foundation "Christ" in verse 11. Then in verse 12, he says this:

> *Now if anyone builds on this foundation with gold, silver, precious stones, wood, hay, straw, each one's work will become clear; for the Day will declare it, because it will be revealed by fire; and the fire will test each one's work, of what sort it is.*

Now, for the sake of scriptural integrity, it is clear that Paul is talking about our work in the kingdom. But I want you to see that we are "building" something on the foundation that is "Christ.". The point is; God is building on Christ, the foundation of our faith.

I dare call framing revelation doctrinal truth. There are times in the scriptures where we see God unveil ideas that help to flesh out the structure of the kingdom. These are most evident in the lives of the Apostles, Peter, and Paul. What I share going forward is going to take listening skill. I am aware of the fact that I am treading on sensitive soil, but may God help me to relay this truth accurately. I also pray that He helps you to interpret my statements correctly.

It is clear that God spoke in a revelatory way to Paul and Peter. And yet, I want you to know that nothing they heard was foundational. Both of them built on the foundation of Christ. The revelation they received is akin to those in the building process who frame the structure. The scriptures confirm this as well. Let's read Ephesians 2:20.

> *Now, therefore, you are no longer strangers and foreigners, but fellow citizens with the saints and members of the household of God, having been **built on the foundation of the apostles and prophets, Jesus Christ Himself being the chief cornerstone,** in whom the whole building, being fitted together, grows into a holy temple in the Lord, in whom you also are being built together for a dwelling place of God in the Spirit.*

See, there is that term "cornerstone" in reference to Christ. There is also mention of the apostles' relationship to that stone. Again, we see a building process. The apostles and prophets (of old) framed the structure. Some people think that the reference to the prophets in the passage points to the New Testament prophets. However, Paul is referring to the apostles building on what they understood from the literary works of the Old Testament prophets. The Old Testament prophets prepared the way for the apostles to frame the structure of the kingdom. The insight gleaned from their literary works, called the scriptures, allowed them to be very effective.

That being the case, the immediate interpretation tells us that the apostles and prophets laid in the framework for our faith. The immediate application is that the early church was to live within the constructs of the apostles' teachings. Likewise, we should not seek to demolish their teachings. Understanding that God is building, however, leads to a broader application. Knowing that God adds line upon line precept upon precept, we know that God is still adding to His house.

Now, I don't believe that we are in the structuring phase of the building process. I do think, however, that God is still building His kingdom. That means that He is still teaching us about Himself. The question is, how does He do this?

I believe that the answer is in the same verse that we hold so dear. 1 Timothy tells us that the scriptures are good for doctrine. Ephesians 2:20, which we read earlier, also unveils how. Most people separate the insights of the apostles from the scriptures. We tend to believe that God spoke to them, and they created scriptures. However, I want to show you something. Ephesians 2:20 tells us that the apostles relied on the prophets. I believe that it is a reference again to the prophets of the scriptures.

Everyone in the New Testament church built his or her doctrines on the scriptures. Even the Chief Cornerstone Himself relied on the scriptures to cement His work in the life of the Church. We see this example in Luke 24:13-32. Jesus appeared to two fellas on the road to Emmaus, as they were reading and pondering the scriptures regarding the Christ. At the time of His appearance, He explained the scriptures to them, though they did not recognize Him. Eventually, after He vanished, they realized that the mysterious man that spoke to them was Jesus. Though Jesus could have unveiled Himself, he didn't. He chose to build upon His foundation by revealing the truth stated in the scriptures. Look at what they said in verse 32.

*And they said one to another, Did not our heart burn within us, while he talked with us by the way, and **while he opened to us the scriptures**?*

I want us to know that God is still opening the scriptures. He is still building upon our understanding. He also used the scriptures to do the same in the life of the apostles. Look at Galatians 4:21-31. It reads:

Tell me, you who desire to be under the law, do you not hear the law? For it is written that Abraham had two sons: the one by a bondwoman, the other by a freewoman. But he who was of the bondwoman was born according to the flesh, and he of the freewoman through promise, which things are symbolic. For these are the two covenants: the one from Mount Sinai which gives birth to bondage, which is Hagar— for this Hagar is Mount Sinai in Arabia, and corresponds to Jerusalem which now is, and is in bondage with her children— but the Jerusalem above is free, which is the mother of us all. For it is written:" Rejoice, O barren, you who do not bear! Break forth and shout, you who are not in labor! For the desolate has many more children than she who has a husband." Now we, brethren, as Isaac was, are children of promise. But, as he who was born according to the flesh then persecuted him who was born according to the Spirit, even so it is now. Nevertheless what does the Scripture say? "Cast out the bondwoman and her son, for the son of the bondwoman shall not be heir with the son of the freewoman." So then, brethren, we are not children of the bondwoman but of the free.

Look at how Paul is used the scriptures to build the framework for the household of God. See, we think of his words as something new. But, his insight is based on what God revealed to him from the scriptures. I also want you to notice the revelatory nature of his understanding. Look at the allegory in verses 24-25. He starts verses 24 with the statement *"For these things are symbolic..."* Then he unpacks an idea that is so complex that you wonder how he came to his conclusion about Sarah and Hagar. In fact, I cannot think of one letter that Paul wrote where he did not expound upon some scripture. He was building line upon line, precept upon precept. We are to do the same. God is still building His household of faith!

Here is another example. What we see in the life of Peter is what scares some people. In Acts 10, Peter had a vision that reshaped the understanding of the faith. Until Acts 10 the Gospel was only preached to the Jewish people. At that point, they believed the Gospel was a national religion, not an international one. Therefore, they did not seek to minister to the Gentiles. Then Peter had a vision that changed everything. It was a doctrinal revelation with significant consequences.

While praying on a rooftop a vision suddenly appeared to him. A voice in the vision challenged him to eat things forbidden by Jewish law. Therefore, being a good Jewish man, he resisted the instructions. It is fascinating to read. What makes it so interesting is the fact that Peter was able to identify the divine nature of a voice that told him to break the law, which God established. As we know, the encounter resulted in the preaching of the Gospel to the Gentile nations.

Before I go further, I need to clarify what God revealed to Peter. There is no doubt in my mind that someone will choose to open themselves to deception by misinterpreting Peter's experience. Did God really tell Peter to do something in opposition to His written word? It certainly appears that way. The voice only seems contrary to the written word if you do not know what else the written word says about the subject. Zechariah established hundreds of years earlier that God was going to open the doors of salvation to the Gentiles. While it certainly appears that God contradicted His word, He did not. He merely brought to pass what He promised in the written record provided by the prophet Zechariah. Look at what he foretold in Zechariah 2:10-12:

> "Sing and rejoice, O daughter of Zion! For behold, I am coming and I will dwell in your midst," says the LORD. "Many nations shall be joined to the LORD in that day, and they shall become My people. And I will dwell in your midst. Then you will know that the LORD of hosts has sent Me to you."

Initially, it appears that Peter heard something new. But,

the vision challenged his perspective so that He could build accurately on the foundation, the work of Christ. Likewise, that truth is supported in scripture.

Proceeding Words
Foundational revelations are cornerstone ideas from God. They set the course for God's work. Framing revelation builds on the idea that God speaks in proceeding words. Some call it "progressive" revelation. Jesus said in Matthew 4:4, that *man does not live by bread alone but by every word that proceeds from the mouth of God.*

To help us understand the difference between the two, here is an example. When God spoke to Moses in Exodus 3:7-10 to tell him to take the people to Canaan, that was a foundational moment in Moses' life. In an instance, Moses' life had a purpose and destination. In teaching on the prophetic, I call that the "cornerstone word." It is God's idea that unveils destiny or direction. Out of that word comes the proceeding word. The proceeding word is progressive in nature. It follows the idea that God builds "here a little there a little." Proceeding words always proceed from the cornerstone word. God's word to Moses about Canaan established his direction, but every following word moved him closer to that goal.

How, how does this all relate to our discussion? God spoke through Jesus to establish the foundations of the household of faith. That was the cornerstone doctrine. Then He spoke to the apostles to frame the household so that it had structure. Those doctrines give us boundaries for our faith. However, God is still building out the interior. That is why He is still speaking. He is teaching us about His ways; His voice; prayer; spiritual warfare; how to operate in His power; and much more. No one can say that we know everything there is to know about God. What we have is foundational truth provided by Jesus, and the framework proceeding from that foundation. It should be further noted that the word doctrine simply means "teaching." I think it is erroneous to say that God is no longer teaching us. What we also fail to realize is that the scriptures merely build upon the foundation of Christ. They tell us who He is, what He did, why He did it, what He expects from us, how the world will end, and where we will live when it does. Still, embedded in the Bible are many ideas upon which we create doctrine (teachings) that progresses our understanding of God's kingdom.

Paul was the most prolific theological mind of his time (as far as we know). Yet, he did not operate in pure revelation. As I showed you, his revelation was rooted in the unveiling of the scriptures. What he really did was expound and expose the truth hidden therein. This is why he tells us that all scriptures were written for our benefit. Again, it should be noted that the scriptures to which he is referring are the Old Testament books; the Torah and the books of the Prophets.

We have now examined two different stages of revelation from God. In our examples, we saw that God spoke to Adam, Abraham, Moses, and Jesus to establish foundational doctrine. We will never see that level of revelation again. If anyone tells you that they have a revelation that establishes a new foundational truth, please run for the hills. It is a demonic doctrine! Then we saw that God spoke to Peter and Paul to elaborate on and illuminate truth hidden in the scriptures. This kind of revelation still occurs. This kind of revelation should fall into God's plan of "here a little, there a little, line upon line." It must fall in line with what God has already said. For that reason, it should always be checked against the whole counsel of scripture. Because this type of revelation is drawn out of the scriptures, it is easy to scrutinize.

Personal Revelation

Finally, there is one other level of revelation to consider. The last level of revelation a person may receive is "personal" revelation. Any legitimate bible scholar should be able to recognize that the majority of God's interaction with those in the scriptures fell into the category of personal revelation. Those personal revelations fall into a few categories. They are guidance, governance, counsel, instruction, and information.

Personal revelations do not establish new foundational truths. Neither do they highlight ideas in the scriptures to bring doctrinal change. Personal revelations are words from God about how to go forward in life. They tell us how to live, bring conviction about our direction, provide specific insight into areas of our life circumstances, unveil our callings, and more. In the bible, this kind of revelation is typical. We should also consider that most of today's prophetic words are personal.

Before we go further, let me clarify the parameters of personal words. The term "personal" does not mean that these words are directed to an individual. The term "personal" describes the nature of the revelation more than the audience it addresses. A personal word can be directed to an individual. It can also be directed towards a group, church, organization, nation, or even the world.

Here are some examples. In Acts 8:26-40, the Holy Spirit speaks to Philip. When he does, he directs him to approach an Ethiopian man sitting on a chariot reading the scriptures. When he obeys, he shares the Gospel with the man. Because of his obedience the man gives his life to Christ. This is an example of a personal word from God that provided guidance. Next, we see God speaking to Paul in Acts 22:17-21. He tells him that He does not have many believers in the town where Paul resides. Knowing that the residents mean to harm Paul, Jesus instructs him to leave. This time the personal proved to be advisory.

Personal words may take many forms. In Philips example, it provided guidance. In Paul's example, it was counsel. In Acts 9:10-15, Jesus speaks to a disciple named Ananias about Paul. His words to him are both directional and comforting. He gave him an assignment and alleviated his concerns about Paul, who previously jailed and killed Christians. We see a similar example in Acts 15:32. In this passage, Judas and Silas, both prophets, speak prophetically to the Church. Their words are described as encouraging and strengthening.

All of these instances show us God's personal revelations at work in the life of believers. Try to imagine these scenarios without God's personal instruction for the situation. It is hard isn't it? Would Christians exist in Ethiopia if God had not given personal direction to Phillip? There is something to think about.

What Paul also Told Timothy

Those in opposition to the idea that God is still speaking neglect certain truths. Most of the time, they recklessly abandon the obvious in pursuit of establishing their argument. For instance, we know that Paul encouraged Timothy to rely on the scriptures. Again, he tells him that they are suitable for everything that he needs to be effective as a man of God.

If we only look at this scripture to draw a conclusion regarding the availability of God's voice, we may find ourselves in error. My argument thus far is that God speaks to us via His Bible and His voice. I have confirmed this many times in the scriptures. I showed us that history bears witness to the two forms of God's voice. Both were consistent elements in the faith community. Israel had the law; they also had the prophets. Likewise, the church had the scriptures (the law and the book of the prophets) and the prophets.

Now, in light of these facts, let's look at this in the life of Timothy. Again, we know that Paul told him to rely on the scriptures, yet, 1 Timothy 1:18 records these words:

> "This charge I commit to you, son Timothy, **according to the prophecies** previously made concerning you, **that by them** you may wage the good warfare..."

Notice the bolded parts of the text. The same Paul that advises the young pastor to rely on the scriptures is also telling him to rely on a prophecy. The contrast in ideas teaches us something foundational. Paul's words unveil to us that each, the scriptures and prophecy, has its own unique role in the believer's life. The scriptures are presented to us as what develops our character. I agree that it is fundamentally wrong to rely on prophecy as a tool of development. The scriptures do not indicate that we should use prophecy in that manner. I have never seen anyone use it that way. Still, that does not mean that it does not happen.

While prophecy is not presented to us as a tool of development, it is put forward as a tool of encouragement and direction. Paul even suggests that it is a viable weapon in spiritual warfare.

Paul had such a respect for prophecy in the church that he wrote these words to the church in Thessalonica:

Do not despise prophecies. Test all things; hold fast to what is good. (Thess. 5:20-21)

Presented again is the notion that Paul believed that the prophetic ministry had a relevant place in the church. For that reason, he provided advice for its use. Moreover, again, we see him promoting prophecy even though they had the scriptures. The point of all of this is to show you that the voice of God and the scriptures have always cohesively worked together. With such clear evidence of such, it begs us to wonder why we believe it should be any different today. If Israel needed the scriptures and the voice of God, and the early Church needed both, why would we not need both of them too? That is something to ponder.

That being said, while am a huge promoter of our need for the verbally expressed voice of God, I am equally pro-Bible. Still, it must be stated again that the scriptures we highly regard never show us that God spoke with the intent of giving us scriptures. The only time we see anything close to such is in the life of Moses. Other than that, men who heard from God thought enough of it to capture its truth. That truth is what we allow to govern our lives. I believe their example enforces the need to hear God's voice.

God Said Everything in the Scriptures

It is simply untrue to say that God said everything He needed to say in the scriptures. Not only is it not true, but it is also unbiblical. In Acts 2:17-18, Peter declared that God is going to speak to the earth in these last days. It reads:

> "In the last days I am going to pour out my Spirit on all flesh. Your sons and daughters will prophesy, your young men will see visions; your old men will dream dreams. Even on my servants, both men and women, I will pour out my Spirit in those days, and they will prophesy."

Peter's declaration is a clear indication that God did not speak with the intent of creating the scriptures. If He did,

He would have only spoken to the appointed men we revere as the authors. Why would God speak to "all flesh" if He intended for only a handful to relay His messages? Just think about that for a second.

I took my time to deal with the stages of revelation to bring us to this point. I wanted you to see that the scriptures are foundational. I agree that we will never experience that level of insight again. We also looked at revelation that unveils the scriptures. This type of insight is available today to those God anoints for the job. I also believe that God opens the scriptures to all believers on a basic level. Then we looked at revelation that is personal. When you consider these three stages of revelation, you realize that personal revelation was abundant. Personal revelation showed the earlier generations how to accomplish God's will. The other thing the scriptures teach us about personal revelation is that God uses His voice to guide us. It shows us that He is intimately involved in aiding us to do His will. Here is something for you to think about: How many people in the Bible completed their task devoid of God's personal instructions for the situation? God used His voice to get Moses and Israel out of Egypt and into Canaan. God used His voice to get Joshua and Israel into the Promised Land. God used His voice to navigate Gideon, Paul, Philip, Samuel, and a few others to their destiny.

Let's look at a few more examples. There was King Abimelech, whom God spoke to warn him about committing adultery. Then there was Balaam, whom God tried to lead away from the misuse of his gifting. There was Nebuchadnezzar, whom God warned about his pride. There was Laban, Jacob's father-in law, whom God also warned about his actions. These are just a few examples of personal words operating in the lives of various individuals. This list does not include the many persons God gave personal prophetic instruction to via a prophet. Every one of these examples teaches us that we are not to exclude God from our personal decisions. Again, I note that He spoke to them by His prophets, though He provided a written law.

The Most Obvious Idea

I think we are kidding ourselves if we believe that God has said everything that needs to be said in the Bible. I know that is a harsh statement. However, before you allow a spirit of offense to settle in your heart, look at what Revelation 11:3-6 says:

> *And I will give* power *to **my two witnesses, and they will prophesy** one thousand two hundred and sixty days, clothed in sackcloth." These are the two olive trees and the two lampstands standing before the God of the earth. And if anyone wants to harm them, fire proceeds from their mouth and devours their enemies. And if anyone wants to harm them, he must be killed in this manner. These have power to shut heaven, so that no rain falls **in the days of their prophecy**; and they have power over waters to turn them to blood, and to strike the earth with all plagues, as often as they desire.*

Pay attention to the bolded text. If God said everything He needed to say already, then what are these two witnesses going to say? Are they going to read from the Bible? What are they going to say that has not already been said? Can you see the inconsistency of this argument yet?

Scriptures at the Heart of the Argument
Finally, I need to address this error by confronting the scripture basis from which it flows. The first scripture to tackle is 2 Timothy 3:16, "All scripture is given by inspiration of God..." Those using this passage to support their belief that prophecy is of no value in today's church argue that it only justifies the authority of scripture. In other words, God's words can only be found in the Bible.

It is an interesting point of view. It even seems to be a substantiable truth. However, when closely examined, we discover that it is founded upon an erroneousness interpretation of the passage. To get to its true meaning I am going to revisit an idea from chapter two—scripture interpretation. By doing so, I am going to lay the groundwork for interpreting the passage. This section will also further serve to help us see other passages as they were meant to be read.

Breaking Down Passages Correctly
When reading the Bible, you must always remember that it addresses a specific people, in specific circumstances, at a specific time in history, and for a specific reason. When its contents are absorbed in that context the reader is able to

get to the immediate interpretation. As defined in chapter two, the immediate interpretation is the understanding that arises from what the writer is addressing at the time the letter was written. In the case of 1 Timothy 3:16, Paul wrote to the New Testament Church about the Old Testament documents. Through his letter he encouraged them to rely on the value of the truth that God provided to nation of Israel's patriarchs.

The immediate interpretation also has an immediate application. The immediate application of the text shows us how those who received the letter should apply the information in it; hence, Paul's instructions to Timothy. Now, of course, we know that the immediate interpretation and application have a broader context. The broader interpretation and application refer to how we, in the new dispensation, are to apply the information to our modern time.

This is where things get off track. We have unfortunately confused what Paul said to Timothy as something meant to be applied broadly. Therefore, we assume that the reference to "all scripture" relates to the New Testament. However, as I noted, Paul's letter is to New Testament believers regarding Old Testament documents. For that reason, this passage cannot be used to justify the belief that God is silent. Neither it is a suitable defense to promote the belief that anything God says is as valuable as the scriptures.

If we hold to such ideas while keeping the passage in context, we invent an unsubstantiated false narrative. If Paul's statement to Timothy excludes any further communication from God, then Paul invalidates his own words. Meaning they are not inspired by God. How can they be, if he believed that he was only to rely on the scriptures? We believe, however, that the whole canon of scripture is a gift from God.

No serious bible scholar can denounce the authenticity of Paul's writings. Some of the most potent ideas in all of the scriptures come from him. It is Paul that tells us how to be saved. He also provides the most substantial information regarding the cross. Paul's writing informs us about spiritual warfare and levels of demonic beings. It is very evident that Paul heard from God quite a bit. We can rest assured that his words were divinely inspired.

2 Timothy 3:16 does not support the idea that God is no longer speaking. Instead, its only point is to show us the profitable truth that God's words are timeless. Pushing it beyond that meaning will only lead to error. Likewise, bad theology leads to bad practices. I dare say that denying God the opportunity to speak is one of those practices and have led to poor consequences.

The next scripture I want to look at is Revelation 22:18-19. It closes with some final thoughts that read:

"For I testify to everyone who hears the words of the prophecy of this book: If anyone adds to these things, God will add to him the plagues that are written in this book; and if anyone takes away from the words of the book of this prophecy, God shall take away his part from the Book of Life, from the holy city, and from the things which are written in this book"

Somehow people imply that John's warning in verse 19, regarding adding to or removing words from "this book," is a reference to the Bible. I even heard a really well-respected and scholarly theologian use this passage to make that point. He thought that John spoke with foresight about a forthcoming book that would encompass what we call the Bible. I was so disappointed in this man. How could he be so well educated and still come to such a farfetched conclusion?

His strange, but common understanding of the passage, beckons us to apply our new insight into scripture interpretation—immediate interpretation and application and broader context and broader application. Revelation 22:18-19's immediate context tells us that John is only referring to the Book of Revelation. That also means that the immediate application is a warning against altering the words of the Book of Revelation. Now, of course, we then extend that truth to the broader context. The broader context teaches us that God thinks very highly of His thoughts, and no one should lightly regard what He says. However, even after looking at the more extensive application, no one can conclude that God is finished speaking. This verse does not lend itself to that idea.

There is one more verse that is commonly abused to support the idea that God finished speaking with the invention of the Bible. 1 Corinthians 13:8-12 reads:

> *Love never fails. But whether there are prophecies, they will fail; whether there are tongues, they will cease; whether there is knowledge, it will vanish away. For we*

know in part and we prophesy in part. But when that which is perfect has come, then that which is in part will be done away. When I was a child, I spoke as a child, I understood as a child, I thought as a child; but when I became a man, I put away childish things. For now we see in a mirror, dimly, but then face to face. Now I know in part, but then I shall know just as I also am known.

This passage is foundational to the myth that God ceased speaking. It is also one of the pillars of the doctrine of cessation. The cessationist doctrine promotes the belief that the Holy Spirit's manifestation gifts, mentioned in 1 Corinthians 12, are no longer operational. Those who champion this idea believe that God's miracles are no longer a normal part of the believer's experience. Normal is the keyword. Cessationists do believe in God's miracle power. However, they do not accept the normalization of such encounters with Him. Likewise, debunking the myth depends on successfully exegeting this key passage. To do so, I must expose the key themes of 1 Corinthians. Once exposed, it is easy to see the fallacy in the interpretation put forth by cessationist teachers.

<u>Looking at the Passage Closely</u>

At first glance, the book of 1 Corinthians appears to have a lot of varied themes. For instance, it talks about spiritual wisdom versus natural wisdom: the carnality of sectarianism behavior: the personal impact of sexual impurity: how the saints should resolve legal disputes: marriage and divorce:

the sacredness of the communion table: understanding spiritual gifts; the uniqueness of each believer in Christ: proper prophetic protocol: and the importance of believing in the resurrection of the dead. Because it covers such a vast array of subjects, it is easy to overlook the significant current that undergirds the entire book. Its many apparent themes also tempt us to examine the individual passages hosting them without considering how they fit into the whole narrative of the book. This type of negligence of study alienates the truth that can only be mined from seeing the whole the book.

The cessationist doctrine undergirding the idea that God is silent fits that description. It invents an interpretation by ignoring the context of the whole book. For instance, they believe this passage foretells the Bible. Their interpretation seems logical, but only if viewed without considering key chapters. Getting a more accurate understanding requires us to start at chapter 1.

Chapter 1
Chapter 1 is vital to understanding Paul's statement. When studying the gifts, most people read chapters 12-14. But, if you start at chapter 12 without considering chapter 1, you will fail to understand chapter 13's concluding idea entirely. In chapter 1, much like a sermon's introduction, Paul prepares the reader for ideas he intends to address in the letter to the Corinthians. As he introduces what he plans to share, he says in verses 4-9:

Common Arguments Against Hearing God's Voice

> *I thank my God always concerning you for the grace of God which was given to you by Christ Jesus, that you were enriched in everything by Him in all utterance and all knowledge, even as the testimony of Christ was confirmed in you, so that you come short in no gift, eagerly waiting for the revelation of our Lord Jesus Christ, who will also confirm you to the end, that you may be blameless in the day of our Lord Jesus Christ. God is faithful, by whom you were called into the fellowship of His Son, Jesus Christ, our Lord.*

This passage introduces four key components needed to comprehend chapter 13's concluding idea. They are utterance, knowledge, gifts, and revelation. As we examine more of the chapter Paul also introduces a fifth element into the equation—dissention. Dissention is at the heart of Paul's motivation for writing the letter. Likewise, the other four components are intricately tied to why the dissention exist. Unveiling their relationship to each other is important to getting the right interpretation of our key passage.

We first see the term utterance in verse 5. It means to express verbally. Next, we see the word knowledge. At the time, the apostle is commending them for being open to receive God's voice. We know this because verse 7a links utterance and knowledge to spiritual gifts; it reads:

> *"...so that you come short in no gift."*

Paul is clearly preparing us for what he shares in 1 Corinthians 12's speaking and revelation gifts. Then he enlightens us further regarding the context of their knowledge in verse 7b. Clearly, the knowledge uttered pertained to Jesus Christ. Verse 7b reads:

> "...eagerly waiting for **the revelation of Jesus Christ**"

Remember that word revelation. It is key to understanding what Paul is addressing in chapter 13:8-12.

These four key words show up in some form throughout much of the letter. Read chapter 2:6-16, 3:1-23, 4:1, 8:1-3, 11:4-5, 12:1, 13:8-11, 14:1-35, and 15. The prevalence, specifically, of the terms utterance or knowledge lead us to conclude that much of the Corinthians' problems stemmed from an issue in these areas. This idea is verified in chapter 1:10-11. They read:

> *Now I plead with you, brethren, by the name of our Lord Jesus Christ,* ***that you all*** <u>***speak the same thing,***</u> *and that there be no divisions among you, but* ***that*** *you be perfectly joined together in the* <u>***same mind***</u> *and in the* <u>***same judgment.***</u> *For it has been declared to me concerning you, my brethren, by those of Chloe's household, that there are contentions among you.*

So far, we know that God blessed the Corinthians with His voice and His knowledge. We also know that the context of God's knowledge related to Jesus Christ. Finally, we know that somewhere along the way conflicting views led to contention among the Corinthians. With this in mind, the rest of the letter falls into place.

For instance, Paul's rebuke to them in chapter 12:3, *"No one call Jesus accursed..."* makes sense. It also clarifies why he spend so much time explaining the uniqueness of their assignments in the Body of Christ. It further clears up why he gave such a detailed explanation of love in chapter 13. Finally, it paints a vivid picture of the need for church order, as outlined in chapter 14.

Looking at Chapter 13

Chapter 13 is affectionately called the love chapter. Again, it also builds on the heels of the problem that Paul felt compelled to address—developing a sense of unity and community. Amid his discussion, Paul encourages the people to operate in a spirit of love, even emphasizing the higher place value of love over spiritual gifts. I Corinthians 13:8 begins the summary of his admonition on love. He wrote: *"Love never fails."*

His next words to them are at the heart of today's confusion about the voice of God and spiritual gifts. It reads:

> *"But whether there are prophecies, they will fail: whether there are tongues, they will cease; whether there is knowledge, it will vanish away."*

Please note those key themes: *utterance* and *knowledge*. Paul's next words allude to the frailty of the utterance and knowledge. They read:

*"For we **know in part** and we prophesy in part."*

If transposed, these verses could read: "For we only have part of the story, therefore, we speak from the little part that we know and understand."

Then he adds:

*"But when that **which is perfect has come**, then that **which is in part** will be done away."*

Up to this point, everyone agrees that the phrase *"that which is in part"* refers to an incomplete revelation or understanding of Christ. The question is, what does *"that which is perfect"* refer to? Cessationists believe it to be a foretelling of a forthcoming book that contains everything we need to know about Jesus. In other words, they believe it refers to the Bible. Likewise, they believe the phrase "that which is in part" refers to prophecy, otherwise noted as God speaking. As noted in the passage, *"that which is in part will be done away with."* With this supposed understanding, Cessationist see no need for prophecy in modern times, especially now that we have a Bible, believed to contain a perfect revelation of Christ. On the surface, it makes perfect sense. But, you must go back to chapter one to get an understanding of what Paul is talking about.

Let's look again at chapter 1. Verse 7 reads:

*"...so that you come short in no gift, eagerly **waiting for the revelation of our Lord Jesus Christ.**"*

One can make many assumptions about the phrase "revelation of our Lord..." Some assume that it refers to knowledge about the Lord. Maybe that is why Paul addresses the spirit of error in 1 Corinthians 12:3 which reads:

Therefore I make known to you that no one speaking by the Spirit of God calls Jesus accursed, and no one can say that Jesus is Lord except by the Holy Spirit.

Obviously, someone in their congregation relayed an inaccurate revelation. Chapter 12 leads us to believe that the revelation refers to imperfect knowledge about Jesus. Still, what were they saying that was so wrong? We will look at the answer later.

Others believe that the phrase refers to the second appearance of the Lord. I think that the phrase is holistic in its presentation. The fact that Paul addresses "utterance and knowledge" frequently lead us to believe that He was referring to imperfect understanding. However, chapter 15 insightfully raises the possibility that Paul was also referring to the second coming. It gives us a glimpse into how the Corinthians called Jesus accursed.

Chapter 15

As previously noted, Paul starts chapter one by talking about utterance and knowledge. Again, He does so in one form or another in many other chapters. One significant place is chapter 15. For now, I want to look at it in light of chapter 12. Again, it is obvious that some of the Corinthians were espousing ideas that were not consistent with the gospel, evidenced by Paul's statement in 1 Corinthians 12:3.

The word accursed means to excommunicate; or to exclude from participation. In other words, someone spoke words in the service that attempted to eliminate the worship of Jesus. The Corinthians were likely victims of the many troubling doctrines of their time. One of them, Docetism, taught that Jesus was never flesh and blood but a spirit. This was a very toxic idea. It struck at the core of what we believe about our Savior. The biggest problem with this teaching is it denies the possibility of a resurrection. Obviously, if Jesus did not really live in a body, then He could not have really died. If He did not die, then He could not rise from the dead. This doctrine also indirectly promoted licentious behavior. By doing so, it denied the Lordship of Jesus Christ.

According to chapter 15 not everyone was teaching error. For that reason, Paul pens these words in 15:12:

...how do some among you say...

Clearly, there was a knowledge gap in the early Church regarding Jesus Christ. That gap in understanding led to disharmony.

Verse 12 also verifies how the Corinthians called Jesus accursed?

*"...how do some among you say that **there is no resurrection of the dead?**"*

Understanding what they were saying helps unveil what the term "revelation of our Lord Jesus Christ" means. To get the gist of the problem, we must read chapter 15 in its entirety.

(Copyright standards prohibits me from posting the chapter in its entirety. Therefore, I will only post sections of text. To get the full understanding of this chapter relative to chapter 1, I implore you to read the full chapter for yourself.)

Verses 15:1-8 read:

Moreover, brethren, I declare to you the gospel which I preached to you, which also you received and in which you stand, by which also you are saved, if you hold fast that word which I preached to you—unless you believed in vain. For I delivered to you first of all that which I also received: that Christ died for our sins according to the Scriptures, and that He was buried, and that He rose again the third day according to the Scriptures, and that He was seen by Cephas, then by the twelve. After that He was seen by over five hundred brethren at once, of whom the greater part remain to the present, but some have fallen asleep. After that He was seen by James, then by all the apostles. Then last of all He was seen by me also, as by one born out of due time.

Verses 12-19 read:

Now if Christ is preached that He has been raised from the dead, how do some among you say that there is no resurrection of the dead? But if there is no resurrection of the dead, then Christ is not risen. And if Christ is not risen, then our preaching is empty and your faith is also empty. Yes, and we are found false witnesses of God, because we have testified of God that He raised up Christ, whom He did not raise up—if in fact the dead do not rise. For if the dead do not rise, then Christ is not risen. And if Christ is not risen, your faith is futile; you are still in your sins! Then also those who have fallen asleep in Christ have perished. If in this life only we have hope in Christ, we are of all men the most pitiable.

After reading chapter 15 we can conclude that Paul's word, *"when that which is perfect has come"* refers to the return of Jesus Christ. The apostle was encouraging them that human error will color the truth until the "revelation of the Lord Jesus Christ," also refers to His second coming.

Knowledge and Immaturity

There is one final element critical to the letter to the Corinthians—maturity. 1 Corinthians 13:11-13 reads:

When I was a child, I spoke as a child, I understood as a child, I thought as a child; but when I became a man, I put away childish things. For now we see in a mirror, dimly, but then face to face. Now I know in part, but then I shall know just as I also am known.
And now abide faith, hope, love, these three; but the greatest of these is love.

These verses pickup on the issues in chapter 1:10 thru chapter 3:1-3. In chapter 1 Paul writes about the division. In chapter 3 he ascribes division to their immaturity.

Look at what the verse says:

And I, brethren, could not speak to you as to spiritual people but as to carnal, **as to babes in Christ.** *I fed you with milk and not with solid food; for until now you were not able to receive it, and even now you are still not able; for you are still carnal.* **For where there are envy, strife, and divisions among you, are you not carnal and behaving like mere men?** *For when one says, "I am of Paul," and another, "I am of Apollos," are you not carnal?*

Then chapter 13 addresses again the subject of maturity. This time, however, it does so in connection to their understanding. Therefore, Paul says, *"For now we see in a mirror, dimly..."* He is referring to their lacking understanding of Christ. We know this by what he says prior to this statement. *"For when I was a child I spoke (utterance) as a child, I understood (knowledge) as a child..."* He continues with, *"Now I know (knowledge) in part..."* Paul was talking to them about their imperfect understanding due to their immaturity. It was their immaturity that hindered them from hearing and relaying the correct information. It is the same thing that hinders us as well.

Each believer has to grow in understanding and discernment. If not, it results in misunderstandings and contentious relationships. This is definitely true today. Modern-day examples are plentiful. Just consider that though we have the Bible, there are still many different ideas about what it says. Hence, this has resulted in thousands of denominations, and even a few cults. All of these examples are the result of our ever-growing understanding of God and has caused many divisions in the Body of Christ.

Organizations such as the Mormons and Jehovah's Witnesses have what they believe to be the correct "revelation." Likewise, it vastly differs from the Protestant Church. Other churches, such as the Catholic Church, the largest Christian denomination, are even considered heretical by most of the Evangelical world. Yet, we all have a Bible from which we draw our conclusions. So, while the Bible is perfect, our understanding is still lacking. The many denominations dividing the Church today, only prove the profoundly prophetic words of God's chief apostle. Yes, we know only part of the truth. Yes, we prophesy according to what we believe is right. For that reason, Paul told the Church in Rome, in Romans 12:7, to prophesy according to their faith. But in the end, whatever we don't know will be known to us when Jesus returns.

One day we will not argue about whether or not a believer should speak in tongues. We won't worry about whether to baptize in the name of Jesus alone, or in the name of the Father, Son, and Holy Ghost. We won't ponder about which day is the Sabbath day. One day our risen King will return, and when He does, all of these arguments will fade away as we come face to face with the God whose shadow we lovingly chase. One day we will fully know the truth. But, until that day, we must examine the scriptures and allow the Holy Spirit to lead us into the truth. It sounds so simple when put that way. People, however, being human and full of fallacy and self-serving desire, make it complicated. Still, our God knows and loves us. For that reason, He is rich in mercy and patience, while we sincerely try to work out His will for each of our lives.

Examples of our Error
We have failed miserably in our attempt to assemble a perfect revelation. Don't get me wrong, God is perfect, that is an undeniable fact. His words are perfect as well. However, His perfection has to flow through our imperfection. For that

reason, Paul states that we, believers in Christ, see dimly. Our lack of clarity is what hinders us from being everything that we can. Still, Jesus will return soon, and all of our gray areas will be clear. For now, though, we are subject to our own limitations. Let's look at a couple of examples of our frailty.

Today, there are many versions of the Bible. There are versions for youth, study versions, plain language versions, and even a Hip-hop version. Some of them are translated from the original Hebrew and Greek texts. Others are watered down versions that attempt to create a more digestible reading experience. To do so, they build a modern language version from those translated for accuracy, such as the King James Version. Amazingly, though created from the same manuscripts, some of them are vastly different from each other. How is such a thing possible? Some preachers even have pet names for some of the translations. For instance, some of them refer to the New International Version (NIV) as the "Non-Inspired Version" Bible. And a vast number of clergy; especially the older saints, refer to the King James Version and the New King James Version as the only authentic version of the scriptures.

There are even controversies regarding the omission of verses from some translations. For instance, I am willing to bet that most Christians are oblivious to the Acts 8:37 controversy. Did you know that some Bible versions intentionally omit this verse of scripture? Let's read it:

So the eunuch answered Philip and said, "I ask you, of whom does the prophet say this, of himself or of some other man?" Then Philip opened his mouth, and beginning at this Scripture, preached Jesus to him. Now as they went down the road, they came to some water. And the eunuch said, "See, here is water. What hinders me from being baptized?" Then Philip said, **"If you believe with all your heart, you may."** *And he answered and said, "I believe that Jesus Christ is the Son of God."*

You may be wondering, "What is the problem?" Well, verse 37 alludes to the idea that we must believe in the work of Christ before being baptized. This means that the practice of baby baptisms is considered a dead work. The belief that baby baptisms is an unacceptable practice is widely taught among Evangelicals. In contrast, a lot of denominations still practice baby baptisms. The omission or addition of this verse depends on where clergymen and women stand on the issue. Therefore, some versions of the scriptures exclude Acts 8:37.

There is also the matter of Bible versions that omit or add books. Did you know that the Catholic Church, the largest Christian denomination, has 14 other books in their version of the Bible? Did you know that the Church in Ethiopia includes the book of Enoch in their version of canonical scriptures? Did you know that the Bible originally had 80 books before it was translated from Latin to English? Are you seeing the impurity of our understanding as it relates to the perfect revelation of God yet? It is painfully evident that we are still looking through a glass dimly. In fact, I dare say that if we saw things clearly, we would not have the schisms that we have today.

Lest the arguments over doctrine seem unique to this era of Church history, please know that it is not. In fact, the Bible highlights two particular groups of Jewish followers, the Sadducees and Pharisees. Each held different theological views about the law. For instance, one believed in the resurrection of the dead. The other did not. This difference was a point of great tension between the two. It is also more evidence of our inability to see past our dimly lit point of views. Consequently, we must all agree with Paul's divine words that tell us that we will eventually see what is hidden from us when Jesus returns for His Bride.

The Sovereignty of God

Don't let your heart be troubled by the different variations of the Bible. I realize that such knowledge can overthrow a person's faith. For that reason, I want to clear up the matter. While it is true that the Bible has changed over the centuries, the substance remains the same. Its value also remains unmatched. When considering its long history, realizing that the Old Testament ruled the Israelites' life for thousands of years, you must appreciate its longevity and popularity. Historically, it is still the best-selling book of all time. Furthermore, its existence meets two basic needs in the Christian community. Those needs have a present-day application for us.

First, what is canonization, why is it important, and how was it done? These are all pertinent questions to answer if we want to understand why some fear the idea of a speaking God. The word *canon* means; rule or measuring stick. It refers to books and writings regarded as *"inspired"* by God and considered authoritative for belief systems and life. 1 Peter 1:21 tells us that prophecy did not come by the *"will"* of man, but holy men of God spoke as they were *"moved/inspired"* by the Holy Spirit. This verse grounds us in the idea that real prophetic words are not the product of human intervention. Likewise, the early Church fathers used this same factor to determine which writings were worthy of entering into the canon. Furthermore, the writings rejected from the canon were deemed products of the human mind and will.

The creation of the Bible was a significant event in Church history. Also, historically, canonization, met and meets two specific needs. 1) it provided unity and solidarity, and 2) it provided boundaries for the truth.

1. ***Unity and Solidarity***

The first five books of the Old Testament called the Torah or Pentateuch were the first books canonized. The books of the prophets followed later. It is believed that the finalized Old Testament probably happened just prior to Christ's birth. At the time, the Jews were scattered among the nations of the world. The creation of an authoritative and singular collection of divine writings created unity among the scattered nation of Israel. Canonizing these books reminded them of their rich history, heritage, and God's faithfulness during a time when they were strangers in a foreign land. This was vital to their survival as a people because in some cases, they lost their language and culture. The Old Testament kept them unified.

The Bible has the same intent today. Teaching us about God is not its sole purpose. It also has the goal of keeping us unified in our faith. It shares with us the rich Jewish history from which our Savior arose. It tells the story of man's sinful condition, the origin of that condition, and God's solution to the problem. Like the scattered Jews, it allows believers across the world, from various counties, cultures, and traditions, to find common ground for our worship of God.

As for the books added later, some Jewish people living outside of the Holy Land embraced approximately 15 other books in addition to the Torah. These were known and the Apocrypha. These are included in the Catholic version of the Bible and are considered inspired works of God. Protestants, however, reject them as inspired though they acknowledge them as valuable. Either way, the goal of scripture is to rally us around one idea, one God, and one faith.

2. **Boundaries for the Truth**

The book of Genesis opens describing the Earth as something without form and void. Notice the order of the words. First, we learn that it has no distinguishable shape. Then we learn that is empty. After learning these facts about the earth, the Bible details how God transformed something useless into something useful. Interestingly, God started the process by establishing order and boundaries. God did not put a single thing on the earth until it had structure. This information tells us a lot about God. In fact, the first thing we learn about Him is that He speaks. Next, we learn that He values order and establishes boundaries. Just consider that He even gave Adam and Eve a boundary.

Boundaries are incredibly vital to the success of anything viable. The New Testament canon was precipitated by arising false doctrines amidst a young growing faith. At the time, there were many writings floating around. As you might expect, not all of them were based in solid truth. Some denied the resurrection. Others denied the truth of Jesus as a physical being. Some imposed impossible limits on the new Christian lifestyle. Many of the Jews struggled to let go of certain traditions in the law to embrace God's grace. According to Paul, two persons even overthrew the faith of many by claiming the resurrection had past (See 2 Timothy 2:18). As you can see, there was a need to bring everything into one place. That said, please understand that creating the canon was not a small or quick accomplishment. It was a major undertaking that took many years and much reflection to decide which writing were valid and which were not. The process was akin to removing weeds from a garden.

I am sure that you can already see the value of the boundaries the Bible creates for us. Just imagine a world where every preacher has a unique revelation from God. That was the reality of those early church days and for that reason every book selected had to meet what is called the requirements of canonicity. This process used five questions as qualifiers for inclusion into the canon. They were:

- Was the book written by a prophet of God?
- Was the writer confirmed by God with signs and wonders?
- Does the message tell the truth about God?
- Did it come with the power of God?
- Was it accepted by God's people (did they have an inner witness of its truth)?

Another question considered is whether or not the writing or the author could be traced back to an apostolic eyewitness. Luke is an example of such a person. He is credited as the author of both the Gospel of Luke and the Book of Acts of the Apostles. He was not one of the original 12 apostles but, he did travel with their ministry. His close proximity to the apostles' ministry lends credence to his testimony.

Finally, the creation of the canon was also, in part, inspired by a man who attempted to add new truth. His teachings and revelations caused the early Church to ask the question, "Can new truth add or change the basic teaching of the Church?" The answer was no! I believe it was this point in church history that caused the minimization of the ministry of the prophet and all forms of prophetic expression. With the restraint of this operation came a resistance to the idea that God is still speaking. For that reason, I wrote about the types of revelation and the reality of our God as a wise master builder. A lot of the principles used to determine what was divinely inspired still applies today.

First, it is true, based on what we know of God as a builder, that no new truth should contradict the foundation that God has already laid. Second, discerning what is of God boils down to does God confirm the message; does the message tell the truth about God; does God bear supernatural witness to its validity; and finally, does it bear witness as truth within the larger scope of God's community. I believe this last one is important. I do not believe that God's people, those who genuinely want His will, are incapable of recognizing His voice. Jesus adamantly declared, "My sheep hear My voice, and they follow Me." In other words, My people know Me when they see and hear Me. I do agree that poor teaching offsets our ability to confidently identify God. Even still, from my experience, most believers have some sense of God's presence and involvement in their life even when the manifestation challenges their belief system.

The Bible is without a doubt a providential work of God. It is perfect and infallible, but those qualities do not negate our human imperfections. The 73-book Catholic version and the 66 Protestant one makes that painfully clear. That is not a slap in our face. It is merely a reality.

Finally, I think that we are deceiving ourselves to believe that God no longer speaks to us. Have you ever read the Bible and had something that you were reading come alive with personal meaning? If so, then you are acknowledging the reality that God speaks. Most believers I know, whether Charismatic or Evangelical, have described this type of encounter with the Bible. That experience is an example of the most modest form of communication with God. No matter how you try to go around it, ultimately it all leads back to the idea that God is still talking.

God spoke audibly in the Old Testament. Now He speaks by the scriptures.

This argument sort of belongs in the category of the last one. However, though it is closely related, I thought I should address it separately.

Somewhere along the way, both those for and against hearing the voice of God came to the same conclusion; They both concluded that God primarily spoke to the Old Testament prophets audibly. Interestingly, there are only a few instances in scripture whereby we can come to that understanding. Such cases are visible in the life of Moses at the burning bush and on Mount Horeb when he received the 10 Commandments. We also have as examples, Adam and Eve. Then there was Cain. There was Noah and just a few others. However, I want you to know that most of the communication between God and His creation, as depicted by the Old Testament, occurred via dreams and visions. In fact, one-third of the whole Bible is dreams and visions. This fact is significant to note because Hebrews 1:1 debunks the idea that the Old

Testament prophets always heard an audible voice. Again, it reads:

> God, who at various times and **in various ways spoke** in time past to the fathers by the prophets,

Notice the wording. It tells us that God spoke in "various ways," not one way. Numbers 12:6-8 sets the foundation of how God spoke most often to the prophets of old. It reads:

> **"Hear now My words:** *If there is a prophet among you,* **I, the Lord, make Myself known to him in a vision; I speak to him in a dream.** *Not so with My servant Moses; He is faithful in all My house. I speak with him face to face, even plainly, and not in dark sayings; And he sees the form of the Lord. Why then were you not afraid to speak against My servant Moses?"*

Pay special attention to the bolded parts. Notice that these are God's words, not Moses' words, regarding how He spoke to the prophets of old. He said, if He were going to speak to anyone, it would most likely be by a dream or a vision. So, God set a precedent with this verse of scripture.

Also, please note that God says that Moses heard His audible voice, even citing that He speaks to him face-to-face. Face-to-face means that Moses saw God when He spoke to him. Likewise, God, Himself calls it rare that He speaks to anyone audibly. Now, let me clear something up. We see many times that people heard the voice of God clearly in dreams and visions. It is clear that there is an internal audible voice and external audible voice. Those who believe God spoke audibly in the Old Testament think that the prophets heard an external audible voice. External is defined as something heard with our natural ears. We know that Moses heard God audibly because everyone saw Moses speak with God face-to-face (See Exod. 33:11). In fact, all of Israel heard God's voice when He spoke from the mountain (See Exod. 19:16-25). But, the truth is that it was, and still is a rare experience. Only Moses, Abraham and the early patriarchs, i.e., Adam, Cain, Noah, a few others, seem to have heard God that way. As for everyone else, according to Numbers 12, they heard Him internally via dreams and visions.

It is essential that I debunk the idea of God speaking "audibly" to the saints of old. "Why," you may ask? Well, most people opposed to the idea of God speaking today think it is preposterous that people hear an audible voice. In their minds, they wonder how something presented as rare in the scriptures is so widespread today. That assumption on their part is wrong. Those of us who hear the voice of God know that we are not listening for a big booming voice from the sky. We have come to realize that God has many ways of speaking to us. Sometimes, though rare, the voice of God is heard as a booming external voice. Sometimes, it is heard as an internal voice, much like the one you hear in your head when reading a book to yourself. Other times, people experience it via a perception. They often "feel" or "sense" that God is saying something to them. Usually, upon sharing their feelings with the intended audience, it is confirmed as accurate. Still, others experience God's voice in dreams and visions. There are a multitude of ways that a prophetic person might experience God's voice. These examples support the truth presented in Hebrew 1:1.

So, if the rationale for rejecting the idea of God speaking today, is founded on the preposterous notion that people are hearing a booming voice from the sky, be at peace. No one is looking for that experience. It was rare in the life of the Old Testament prophets, and it is rare today.

Don't Risk Being a False Prophet

Here is one that really keeps people at bay regarding hearing God's voice. For some people, the idea of prophesying means risking being put to death when the prophecies fail to come to pass. This fear is rooted in Deuteronomy 18:14-22. It reads as follows:

> *The nations you will dispossess listen to those*
> *who practice sorcery or divination. But as for you,*
> *the LORD your God has not permitted you to do so.*
> *The LORD your God will raise up for you a prophet like*
> *me from among you, from your fellow Israelites. You*
> *must listen to him. For this is what you asked of*
> *the LORD your God at Horeb on the day of the assembly*
> *when you said, "Let us not hear the voice of the LORD our*
> *God nor see this great fire anymore, or we will die."*

Is God Still Speaking?

> *The Lord said to me: "What they say is good. I will raise up for them a prophet like you from among their fellow Israelites, and I will put my words in his mouth. He will tell them everything I command him. I myself will call to account anyone who does not listen to my words that the prophet speaks in my name. But a prophet who presumes to speak in my name anything I have not commanded, or a prophet who speaks in the name of other gods, is to be put to death." You may say to yourselves, "How can we know when a message has not been spoken by the Lord?" If what a prophet proclaims in the name of the Lord does not take place or come true, that is a message the Lord has not spoken. That prophet has spoken.*

As you can see, this passage is quite overwhelming. Some suggest that the severity presented warrants not risking speaking for God at all. I will admit that this passage hangs over your head when you say the words, "God said." I don't think anyone can argue with the fact that God cautions us to be mindful when saying, "Thus says the Lord God." However, I'm not sure why we allow our fear in this regard to minimize this aspect of ministry. It is as if we believe that excluding the gift of prophecy removes the sense of responsibility in speaking what is right. However, I think it is important to note the error of such thinking. Whether or not you say, "God said," you are still accountable for His words in the Bible.

For instance, James 3:1 encourages us to approach teaching with a sense of reverence. He warns us all that this position should be sought with the understanding that teachers will receive a stricter judgment. Maybe it is just me, but this sounds like a warning to take seriously! The idea that removing the words "God said" from our vocabulary as a way to escape the penalty for a loose tongue is erroneous. How many times have we heard preachers exegete a passage with the sole purpose of sharing what God said? That is the point of preaching and teaching, is it not? Is it not to tell people what God said to the saints of old? Is it not to use what God said to them as truth that we can apply today? The only difference between the traditional preacher and the prophetic preacher is this; one says what God has said, and the other preaches what God is saying. Either way, the purpose of preaching is to communicate with God's people on His behalf. That being the case, no one is off the hook as it relates to Deuteronomy 18.

Here is something to think about; Sometimes, even within the prophetic movement, people are cautious about saying, "God said." They prefer to use more digestible terms such as "I feel like God is saying..." or "I believe God is saying..." The goal is to avoid putting complete ownership of the words on God. In theory, not doing so lessens the burden on the prophetic vessel. I believe that this practice is okay when learning to prophesy. However, as time goes on, you come to realize that your words matter to the people of God.

One thing that we must come to realize is that preachers have significant influence. Martin Luther King, Jr. shaped history as a preacher. Likewise, many great men and women have impacted the lives of many with the words from their mouth. Regardless of how dishonored the preacher in America has become, people still turn to one in times of trouble. When America experienced the tragedy of 911, church attendance was at an all-time high. People did not go for the fellowship. They turned to the church, hoping that the preacher had an answer to their pain. That was an eye-opening moment for me. It let me know the weighty responsibility of preaching.

What is a preacher? A preacher is what it has always been; a representative for God: A mouthpiece for the Almighty. That understanding is not mine alone. Many unbelievers have that same expectation. For that reason, many of them hold preachers to higher standards than powerful politicians. That is how respected preachers are in society.

Now, if the world puts so much value in the preacher as God's servant and representative, what makes us think we can casually say things and not give an account for those words? Whether you say, "God said" or "God is saying." You are still accountable for speaking as a representative of God. There is no escaping the weighty nature of the preacher's calling.

Here is the point: The person or preacher who believes that God is not speaking today is no safer than the one that does. Both are presumed to be representing God's viewpoint; moral views, political views, humanitarian views, religious views, and more. That being the case, whether he or she preaches from the Bible or by the Spirit, both will give an account for saying, "God said!" Furthermore, anytime you say, "The Bible says..." it is the same as saying God said! Likewise, if your interpretation is wrong, then you are essentially doing the very thing Deuteronomy warns us not to do.

What is the Biblical Definition of a False Prophet?

Something that keeps us from saying the words, "God said," is the fear of being labeled a false prophet. Preachers and laypersons alike share this fear. It is a legitimate fear. It is such a concern that even the Bible addressed it in several places. In fact, most of the prophets wrote about the issue. Even Paul addressed the problem in his writings. Moses also confronted the problem. Finally, the Master Himself, Jesus, addressed the issue. That tells us that we should take a serious look at the problem. I am very much pro-prophecy. Yet, I am equally opposed to false prophets.

Before I go any further, I need to alert you to the fact that there are two primary ways to identify false prophets. First, identify them by their message. By listening to their message, we can discern whether they point us to God or some other deity. Second, we recognize them by their fruit.

The Message: The Divine Brand

Deuteronomy 18:20 lays the foundation for every minister's message. It conveys to us that the prophet's message can be discerned by its central theme. In other words, what is he or she saying?

God has never had a problem finding preachers. Today preachers are abundant. Likewise, they were plentiful in biblical times. His biggest problem was finding those who would consistently communicate His brand.

I am a graphic designer by trade. Therefore, I hear the word "brand" quite often. The success of a business and or campaign depends on consistent messaging. If a company preaches several conflicting messages about its products, customers start to lose faith in the company. That is why ensuring that everyone at the company understands the message is vital. The same is true in God's kingdom. If He is to be successful, then He knows that His success depends on everyone saying the same thing. It would be counterproductive for one preacher to say adultery is sin, while another encourages it. Don't you agree that such would be confusing? Well, God experienced such problems in biblical times. He often spoke to confront the inconsistent messaging of the false prophets. He did so because their messages promoted the worship of false gods.

That being the case, God tells us that the main attribute of a false prophet is his false message. False prophets proclaim the glory of other gods. They preach against God's brand. Therefore, we need to ask the right questions about the prophet's message. Is it consistent with God's kingdom-brand? Finally, does it call us to serve other gods?

The Fruit

The next thing that assists us in identifying false prophets is their fruit. Many places in the scriptures refer to fruit. The most important of them comes from Jesus. He said in Matthew 7:15-20:

*"Beware of false prophets, who come to you in sheep's clothing, but inwardly they are ravenous wolves. **You will know them by their fruits.** Do men gather grapes from thornbushes or figs from thistles? Even so, every good tree bears good fruit, but a bad tree bears bad fruit. A good tree cannot bear bad fruit, nor can a bad tree bear good fruit. Every tree that does not bear good fruit is cut down and thrown into the fire. Therefore by their fruits, you will know them.*

1. *Fruit of the Character*

When reading this passage, most people conclude that the lifestyle of the prophet is the subject of Jesus' reference. It is true, though, that someone who represents the Lord should have evidence of His nature. Galatians defines the nature of the Holy Spirit for us. It reads:

But the fruit of the Spirit is love, joy, peace, longsuffering, kindness, goodness, faithfulness, gentleness, self-control.

To grasp the full context, start reading at verse 16. It encourages us to walk in the nature of the Spirit so that we don't satisfy the lusts of our fleshly nature. Then verses 19-21 define those behaviors that are kin to the fleshly nature. Everything listed is an indication of how we are to live. So, we know that God cares about how we live, and the prophet is no different.

2. Fruit of the Followers

While I agree that Matthew 7:15-20 is a reference to character, I also think there is a deeper meaning. I want to submit that the reference to fruit also refers to the lifestyle of the prophet's followers. Jesus wants us to consider how the message affects our lives. Does it drive us to do wickedness? Or, does it lead us into paths of unrighteousness?

We often think of the prophet's message as harmless, yet, the scriptures never present such a point of view. Over and over again, the scriptures show God complaining about prophets whose words have turned Israel's hearts to falsehood and sinful living. Here are a few of those scriptures. Isaiah 9:15-16 reads:

The elders and dignitaries are the head, the prophets who teach lies are the tail. Those who guide this people mislead them, and those who are guided are led astray.

The most considerable evidence of this idea is found in the passage that is foundational to operating in prophetic ministry. God says in Deuteronomy 13:1-5, that we know the prophet is from God by the fact that what he or she preaches inspire us to live righteously. Let's look at it:

"If there arises among you a prophet or a dreamer of dreams, and he gives you a sign or a wonder, and the

sign or the wonder comes to pass, of which he spoke to you, saying, 'Let us go after other gods'—which you have not known—'and let us serve them,' you shall not listen to the words of that prophet or that dreamer of dreams, for the L*ORD* *your God is testing you to know whether you love the* L*ORD* *your God with all your heart and with all your soul. You shall walk after the* L*ORD* *your God and fear Him, and keep His commandments and obey His voice; you shall serve Him and hold fast to Him. But* **that prophet or that dreamer of dreams shall be put to death, because he has spoken in order to turn you** *away from the* **L***ORD* *your God, who brought you out of the land of Egypt and redeemed you from the house of bondage, to entice you from the way in which the* L*ORD* *your God commanded you to walk. So you shall put away the evil from your midst.*

Pay special attention to verse 5. The judgment against the prophet concerns the fruit of the message. Again, when judging the validity of prophecy, sermons, and teachings, we must ask the question, 'Does this message inspire me to walk in God's ways?'

Another aspect of this principle forces us to look not only at our fruit, but what the teaching produces in the life of those who apply it. The passage uses the analogy of a tree and fruit. The tree is the prophet. The fruit is the result of his or her words. What kind of followers does the teaching produce? Jesus is clear that a Christian prophet will produce Christ-like disciples; whereas, a false prophet, such as Baal's prophets, will produce followers of Baal. True words from God, spoken by a real man or woman of God, positively affect how we live.

Finally, Jeremiah 23 shows us yet again the power of God's word to impact the way we live: (emphasis on verses 21-23)

> *"I have not sent these prophets, yet they ran.*
> *I have not spoken to them, yet they prophesied. But if*
> *they had stood in My counsel, and had caused My people*
> *to hear My words, then they would have turned them*
> *from their evil way and from the evil of their doings.*

It is clear that God's voice causes us to live an upright life. I am always leery of doctrines that lead believers to embrace a sinful lifestyle. I am equally as concerned about teachings that hinder the forward movement of the Church. While we should not embrace sin, our teachings should reflect the elements of grace and mercy. If we carefully present the truth with balance, the people will live that way. Then again, that only comes by allowing God to speak His truth into our life.

3. Fruit of the Message: Fulfillment

The last indicator of a real prophet is found in Deuteronomy 18:21-22. It reads:

> *You may say to yourselves, "How can we know when a*
> *message has not been spoken by the Lord?"* ***If what a***

prophet proclaims in the name of the LORD *does not take place or come true, that is a message the* LORD *has not spoken. That prophet has spoken presumptuously, so do not be alarmed.*

The bolded part of the text speaks, yet again, to the idea of fruit. Let's review. There is fruit that results in good character. There is fruit in how we are driven to live out the word of God. Lastly, there is fruit in the fulfillment of the message. If I tell you I planted an apple tree, but an apple tree never grows, then something is wrong. Some read Deuteronomy 18 only considering its implications related to foretelling. However, there is a broader meaning. The overall principle of the passage promotes the idea that God supports His messages. A sermon about deliverance should lead to deliverance. A prophecy that declares a miracle should produce a miracle. In other words, we discern the validity of the prophet's message by the results. Does God confirm the word by causing the hearer to experience the message? That is the question we need to ask.

Here is an example of that truth. Look at what God tells Isaiah about His word in Isaiah 55:10-11. It reads:

As the rain and the snow come down from heaven, and do not return to it without watering the earth and making it bud and flourish, so that it yields seed for the sower and bread for the eater, so is my word that goes out from my mouth: It will not return to me empty, but will accomplish what I desire and achieve the purpose for which I sent it.

This passage reveals to us the certainty of God's word. He clearly tells us that anything He says will produce the desired results.

In my book, *You Can Hear the Voice of God Clearly,* I write about the differences between the Shepherd and the hireling. One thing I note is the fact that the Shepherd's voice produces freedom for the sheep. They experience so much freedom that they are comfortable following him. When true prophets speak, people are encouraged to follow Jesus freely. The hireling, however, is not interested in the freedom of the sheep. He only wants to keep them in the pen. His words hinder, bind up, and stop the progress of the sheep.

<u>What a False Prophet is Not</u>

Before I close out my thoughts on this subject, I need to address one more idea. Many people label false prophets such because of bad teaching. The difference between a false prophet and a true prophet is motive. It is possible to teach error while doing so with pure intentions. I do not know many preachers who are without fault in this area. Regardless of how great, insightful, wise, and knowledgeable they are, they are all prone to error.

There is, however, a prophet that intentionally seeks to deceive God's people. When we look at figures like Daddy Grace, David Koresh, and others, we see an intent to deceive, manipulate, and control others. Jesus calls these kinds of prophets "sheep in wolves clothing." He even goes further, saying they are "inwardly" ravenous (Matt. 5:15). The word inwardly refers to their motives. This affirms for us that some preachers seek to espouse false doctrine to deceive others, while others merely teach error. Galatians 2:4 speaks of such persons; people who operated in the Galatian church with the intent to cause problems. Now, let me say that I am not attempting to minimize erroneous teaching. History bears witness that such behavior can lead to horrible consequences. Therefore, we must address error in doctrine swiftly and aggressively. However, error alone does not constitute the label, false prophet.

Apollos is a great example of this truth. His story is found in Acts 18:24-28. This passage of scripture tells us that Apollos was a great teacher. It also shows us that he had a problem. When Paul met him, he was teaching what was then called "The Way" now referred to as Christianity. Verse 25 tells us that he taught the way accurately. Then verse 26 tells us that Aquilla and Priscilla took him aside to explain "the way" more accurately. Notice what seems to be an apparent contradiction. Was Apollos teaching it accurately or inaccurately? The last few words of verse 25 holds the key. It says that Apollos only knew the baptism of John. It reports that he taught "that" aspect of repentance accurately. Aquilla and Pricilla taught him the rest.

Imagine hearing a sermon today from a preacher that only preached the baptism of John, but not the resurrection of Christ. Today, Apollos would be labeled a false prophet, though he was not. The passage teaches us that sometimes error is the result of ignorance, not the malicious intent to deceive. It also humbles all of us preachers and allows us to know that we may not know everything we think we know. It promotes the character trait of being teachable.

Overall, Apollos story validates the fact that teaching something wrong, does not constitute calling someone a false prophet. Again, a false prophet is one who seeks to use a message in God's name to deceive the hearer and lead them away from the one true God.

Common Arguments Addressed

These are the primary arguments preventing some from embracing prophecy in the modern church. As you can see, most of them are unsubstantiated. They lack biblical integrity, and in some cases, are merely nonsense. I believe that they are more rooted in fear than Christ. As I close out this chapter, I plead with you to consider everything you have read thus far. So many people are missing out on the best part of Christianity. Likewise, most of it is due to one or more of the misunderstandings mentioned in this chapter.

Chapter 6

Addressing Our Fear of Deception

How should we address the genuine threat of deception? This question is probably the most important to answer. While writing this book, I tried my best to honestly look at both sides of this issue. I don't think we can ignore the reality of the possibility of deception. As I stated earlier in this book, many religions started on the heels of a false vision, dream, or voice. Likewise, many people have been hurt by such errors. That being the case, we must take a sincere look at how to protect ourselves.

Let me say that protecting ourselves cannot be synonymous with removing ourselves. Some people think that the best way to protect us from erroneous spirits is to remove ourselves from the idea that God speaks. The notion that "excusing ourselves protects us" is the prevailing thought behind the idea that we can only hear from God via the scriptures.

However, removing ourselves does nothing more than stagnate us. Someone once said that the only thing necessary for evil to prevail is for good people to do nothing. The quote implies that anything left to itself will grow. Do we really want errors in doctrine and practice to grow? Do we want people to be deceived? If not, then we must resolve in our hearts to do something that will produce real safety. You say, "What actions should we take?" Here are a few suggestions to help.

#1 Try Education, Not Eradication

I think most of us can agree that bad prophetic ministry is problematic. Victims of such, like pastors and church leaders, in response to bad experiences, often develop negative feelings about prophetic ministers. Furthermore, these feelings tend to lead to unfavorable actions toward such ministries. The most common reaction is to bar the prophetic from the church. Sometimes they go a step further and go after the prophetic person. Their decision to completely disassociate with all things prophetic usually results in painful encounters between prophetic people and those that interact with them. Soon after, the prophet leaves their church, and the prophetic ministry dies. Sometimes the wounded prophetic person leaves in search of a new home for his or her gift. Other times, they quit attending a traditional church setting, settling for online ministry. Finally, some of them completely leave the church and use their gifts for other ungodly purposes.

While grievous errors leave some leaders sour and uninterested in the prophetic aspect of Christianity, we must acknowledge a few things. One, errors need to be addressed. God will more than likely raise up another prophetic voice from within the congregation. When He does, the leaders need to be prepared. We have come to think that ignoring a problem is a good way to resolve one; though, I must say that I have never seen a neglected problem solved. Usually, it got worse. Paul said in Galatians 5:9 that a little leaven leavens the whole lump. That means that anything we ignore will grow until it becomes cancerous to the group.

Second, error is a sign of ignorance. It reveals a lack of education and training regarding the gift. Ignoring the problem is the worst thing a leader can do. It leaves prophetic people to learn about their supernatural gifting on their own. Considering such circumstances, one can hardly be surprised by the problems that arise.

So, if extradition and eradication are not good solutions to the problem, then what is? The best solution to a dilemma of ignorance is education.

The Apostle Paul faced this very same situation in the church at Corinth. 1 Corinthians 12:1 reads:

> "Concerning spiritual gifts brethren, I do not want you to be ignorant. No man speaking by the Spirit of God calls Jesus accursed. And no one can say that Jesus is Lord except by the Spirit."

Notice that Paul is addressing the idea that someone in the church is operating in the demonic. We know this by the fact that he informs them of the difference between a person speaking for God and a person who is not. Also, please notice how he decides to address this concern. He says, in light of what we see going on, I don't want you to be ignorant concerning these spiritual matters. Paul concludes that the best way to tackle the issue is to teach them the right way. Consequently, he writes three chapters detailing for them how the gifts should operate; addressing such things as the proper motive, proper protocol, ministerial order, and more.

One of my most significant issues with most churches that complain about having members that are "spooky" or "deep" or "super-spiritual" is that they have often provided no place to train those called to these gifts. If a person feels called to evangelism, there are a plethora of classes on the subject. If a person is called to pastoring, again there are college courses galore to train them in that calling. If a person is called to teach, there are any number of unlimited classes on the subject. If a person is called to the apostolic, there are many courses and classes on starting churches and doing missionary work. But how many churches offer classes and conferences for those of us called to the prophetic? Most church leaders would say, none! Yet, we expect people without training to operate effectively and efficiently in the local body. How does that work? It doesn't!

Here is something to think about; While prophetic gifts are despised, they are resident in specific believers by the delegation of the Holy Spirit. It is through His wisdom that prophetic people are called. No one can choose to be prophetic. Only God can call and equip us with prophetic gifting. That said, how is it that leaders feel justified in ignoring and shunning these gifts? How will they answer for telling God to take those gifts out of their churches? Rejecting these gifts shows a distain for the wisdom of God's Spirit. Let that sink in for a moment!

Most pastors and leaders understand the high cost of overseeing souls. The author of Hebrews appeals to believers to submit to leadership because they will have to answer for the souls they shepherd (See Heb. 13:17). Sometimes I think leaders forget that they will also give an account for the souls of the prophetic people as well.

#2 Learn to Discern

Why do we fear the supernatural? Think about it. What is it about it that we fear? Just consider that we have a Bible that was received via dreams, visions, and voices. Likewise, it details for us, God raining down fire in response to a man's prayer. It shows us God opening the Red Sea for Israel to walk across dry ground. It tells us that God defeated thousands of soldiers with 300 men. It tells us of a man with supernatural strength. It conveys the end of the world in detail. With all of these stories about the supernatural nature of God, why are we so fearful? I wonder how being afraid of such is even possible. Even our Gospel is supernatural. It is so otherworldly that Paul acknowledges that it is foolishness to the world (See 1 Cor. 1:18). Have you ever considered how foolish the Gospel sounds? Let's look at it.

Is God Still Speaking?

Humanity got himself into trouble when a talking serpent convinced him to eat fruit from a forbidden tree. The offense so angered God that He condemned all of humanity. To remedy the problem, God sent Himself as the ransom for our sins. To do so, He entered into a virgin named Mary. Mary then gave birth to a baby that we know as God in the flesh, or Jesus. Jesus grows up and travels abroad healing the sick, casting out invisible evil spirits, and raising the dead. To cap it all off, He dies on a cross then raises Himself back to life from the grave. By doing so, He saves all of mankind from their sins. Still, that is not the entire story. The finale, captured by the penned words in Acts chapter 1, reveals yet another layer of the story. In this chapter, Jesus returns to heaven in a cloud. As He ascends, two male ghosts with him tell Jesus' followers that He is going to return in like fashion. That is our Gospel story. It is what we preach and what we/I proudly believe. However, it is a foolish sounding story. It is so silly that it takes faith and grace to believe it. Have you ever thought about the fact that you cannot believe the Gospel without God-given faith? The Bible declares that God has given to each man a measure of faith (See Romans 12:3). Faith to believe the Gospel comes from God. Why? God provides us with faith because of the foolish nature of the Gospel.

If you can believe the Gospel, which is as supernatural of an event as they come, why can't you consider that God is still speaking to us? Do you want to know what I surmise to be the root of our unbelief? Our fear is not rooted in ignorance alone. It is also not rooted in our logical assessments and misinterpretations of scriptures. It is rooted in fear. It is grounded in the reality that most people cannot discern God. Discern means; to distinguish between. Most Christians cannot tell the difference between God and Satan. That is the reality at the core of the opposition to anything supernatural. It is easier to call everything the devil. That way, we falsely convince ourselves that we are safe from deception. But, as I noted in my introduction, many have been deceived by those unskilled in interpreting scriptures. I have never met a Jehovah Witness that used a vision or dream in their evangelism tactics. The only tools they use are a Bible and a written document based in misquotes from the Bible. Likewise, I have seen Christians turn away from the real Gospel to embrace their version of it. In fact, some believers are turning to the Gospel of Inclusion; also promoted by the misuse of scriptures. So, our real problem is that we cannot distinguish God from Satan. I know that is a harsh reality to embrace, yet, you must take my point seriously. I even recommend that you pause right here and reflect on why you fear hearing from God. If you do, I am sure you will come to the same conclusion.

What then is our recourse? I said it in the last section; education is better than eradication. Empower yourself through knowledge. Hosea 4:6 says that we perish for lack of knowledge. Proverbs 29:18 also echoes this sentiment. It says, "Where there is no vision, the people perish." One version of the Bible replaces "perish" with "cast off restraint." In other words, this verse says that without the prophetic word (divine insight and knowledge of God) about our situation, we are likely to operate without boundaries. Is that not what motivates us to preach from the Bible in the first place. That is the majesty of the scriptures. They provide us with boundaries for our lives. However, I want you to know that though Israel had the law. God still considered them to be rogue without His voice. That is something to consider.

There are many good books on the market today that cover hearing God's voice. I recommend mine, "**God, is that You, Me, or the Devil?** Also, **You Can Hear the Voice of God Clearly**. Both are excellent resources that present the subject with balance. Likewise, they have a heavy emphasis on principles of discernment. Being able to confidently identify the voice of God is the key to safety.

#3 Find A Balance

At no point in time should a person be so invested in the idea of God speaking prophetically to them, that they neglect the scriptures. I have been guilty of this very thing many times. Likewise, I found that a closed Bible equals the closing of God's mouth.

One thing that will aid us in finding balance is understanding why God speaks. Do you know why God does supernatural things? Believe it or not, there are reasons for God to speak and do the supernatural. Not understanding those reasons leads to error and imbalance. We talked about a few things when I addressed the subject of personal revelation. But, in the broader context of the supernatural, there is more to see.

God speaks to us because He loves us and wants to inform

us of something: to direct us, or to remind us. These are all great reasons for God to speak to us, but overall, anything supernatural has one goal. That goal is to glorify God. God does supernatural things, to includes speaking to us, to glorify His name.

I am a person who believes in balance. I guess that is why I am writing a book that promotes both reading the Bible and prophecy. I think that the most significant error of the Church in our day is the lack of balance. One group thinks we should have services with no human oversight. Another group feels that we should keep the service rooted in the program. One person believes that God does not do this. Another group thinks that God does the polar opposite. Often, our arguments are so far to one side that we lack a meaningful center. I have learned that God is usually somewhere between our extremes. I am not writing to fight for the prophetic. I am also not writing to fight for the validity of scripture. I am writing to fight for a balanced understanding of our need for both.

The Bible says that God hates an unjust weight (Prov. 11:1). It even goes as far as calling it an abomination. God wants us to have a center. He wants us to know that His voice is multifaceted. It is full of variety and mystery. That is why we need the Bible. It makes the unveiling of the mystery easier. Ultimately, it leads to us walking closer to God in a way that we hear His voice and recognize it as His. Simply put, we need both to be balanced.

#4 Be Realistic

We must acknowledge the reality that the possibility of deception exists for both those who support the prophetic and those who are strictly Bible readers. By allowing ourselves to accept the potential of this reality, we protect ourselves. It is really hard to sneak up on someone that is actively watching for danger. Being realistic about the possibility of deception keeps us on our toes. It awakens our senses and makes us available to wisdom.

In the 7th chapter of the Book of Joshua, the man of God does something interesting. What he does really helps to make my point. At the time, he had just won the war against the city of Jericho. Most of us know that story well. Following his victory at Jericho he also defeated a little town called Ai. These victories were monumental and instrumental in striking fear into the hearts of those God called Israel to dispossess. Israel was on a roll, conquering anything in their way. Their success was primarily due to Joshua's ability and willingness to hear from God. It is a really fascinating read as we see God speaking to him to unveil new strategic ways to take each city.

Israel was so impressive that word of their powerful God spread throughout the known world. Every king in the land stood in horrid fear of Israel because of God. Therefore, five of them came up with a different kind of war strategy. They decided to alter their appearance and deceive Joshua. To do so, they traded their luxurious robes for shabby garments. They also collected old moldy bread to give the impression of having traveled from afar. When they presented themselves before Joshua, they made their strike. This behavior was unconventional warfare. They did not strike Joshua with a spear, sword, or any other kind of weapon. They hit him with a lie. All of a sudden, Joshua was at war, only he didn't know it. Soon after, he made a deal with them to spare their lives. Then he learned that they were of the people he was supposed to destroy. He discovered that they were not beggars, but neighboring kings who lived among the people God appointed for destruction.

Here is what makes the story interesting. Joshua 9:14-15 says:

> *Then the men of Israel took some of their provisions;* ***but they did not ask counsel of the Lord****. So Joshua made peace with them, and made a covenant with them to let them live; and the rulers of the congregation swore to them.*

I can only assume that the last success became the enemy of his future. Like so many of us, he got comfortable and let his guard down. He reminds me of the Church today. Now that we have a Bible, we think we are safe. We don't need to hear from God anymore; we got this." That is what we tell ourselves, consciously, and unconsciously. However, it is a lie. While the scriptures are an invaluable source of good living, we still need the voice of God to speak to us in a personal way to resolve our unique problems.

Joshua had the law. In fact, God told him to meditate

on it for success. Still, nothing in the law prepared him for this moment. The result was deception. Furthermore, please note that the story does not attribute his failure to a lack of knowledge regarding God's written word. Instead, it notes his failure to seek God's personal advice for the situation. This story illustrates the truth that we must be realistic about the reality and possibility of deception. That is true for both the prophetic person and those who oppose the prophetic.

#5 Practice Precaution

One reason we are so fearful is that we fail to follow biblical protocol. That is; we fail to surround ourselves with great counselors. Great counselors are those who can discern. Furthermore, please note that even you strictly Bible teachers should be submitting your sermons to the scrutiny of qualified persons. No one is exempt from error, but we can catch them if we practice Paul's advice in 1 Corinthians 14.

I would also like to add that practicing precaution also means two things: 1) following scriptural protocol and 2) deferring to the scriptures. Operating without these two is a recipe for confusion and failure.

Protocol

As we aspire to embrace the reality of a God who speaks to us today, let us do a few things. One, we need to embrace the idea that God is a God of order. Likewise, there cannot be order where there is no protocol. One reason people are fearful of prophecy today centers around the truth that many prophets minister in a disorderly way. It is not unusual for people in certain circles to randomly break out into prophecy. I know, because I was one of those persons.

In my early days, I made many mistakes. I often, in my pride, spoke out of turn or spoke over others. I assumed that my revelation was more magnificent than theirs. These days, I just sit back and watch. I've learned that God will call on me when He needs me. I cannot tell you how order contributes to an atmosphere of peace and harmony.

Paul has a lot to say about this issue. In fact, he asks in 1 Corinthians 14:26:

> *"How is it then brethren? Whenever you come together, each of you has a psalm, has a teaching, has a tongue, has a revelation, has an interpretation."*

Paul's question to the Corinthians is about order. Oh, how many times I saw groups like this one. He then goes on to provide them an orderly solution for conducting service. After all of his instructions, he closes the subject with these words, *"Let all things be done decently and in order."*

Between his question and his final instruction regarding the matter, Paul gives some guidance regarding prophetic operation in the church. He said:

Limit those speaking to two or three persons. There is nothing more chaotic than seeing a bunch of people prophesying. Again, I have taken part in this type of behavior. Therefore, I am speaking from experience.

Paul tells the Corinthians to appoint those who will be used by God in the service. (*I could say a lot about this point, but I will save it for the next book.*) Now, I remind you that this is after Paul asks the question, *"How is it that when you come together everyone has a psalm, a revelation...)* So, His instructions are to establish order in the prophetic.

I deal with the flipside to this in more detail in number 2. Having an appointed speaker has enormous protective ramifications. While the appointment of speakers limits chaos, it also stifles showoffs! Notice that the passage does not call for a one-person minimal, regarding the appointed speaker. In contrast, it calls for a minimum of two speakers. That means that prophetic people must learn how to share the spotlight.

Not long ago a prophet made a set of predictions, none of which came to pass. It was not the first time he was wrong. There were plenty of other times where he missed God. In fact, I stopped listening to him because he was unreliable. His preaching was great. His personal prophecies were spot on. However, his corporate prophetic words regarding world events were terrible. After a while, I started wondering how this was possible. Then God brought to mind that the prophet is always allowed to operate without order. No one ever judged his words. No one else ever spoke but him. Likewise, his error led to a period of worldwide persecution.

Let those prophetic people who sit by judge the validity of the prophecy. This has to be one of the most important

Addressing Our Fear of Deception

protocols to implement. It is imperative that we ensure that we appoint those who can judge prophecy. According to the scriptures, one of two people is qualified to do so. They are prophets and spiritual people. That means that prophecy is primarily judged by prophets. The Bible also shares with us that a "spiritual" person can judge prophecy. We first see this idea in I Corinthians 14:29, where Paul writes, speaking of the prophet, *"...and let the others judge."* We also have a biblical reference to the "spiritual" person. Chapter 14:37 reads:

> *"...if anyone considers himself to be a prophet **or spiritual person**, let him acknowledge that what I am writing comes from the Lord.*

1 Corinthians 14:29 and 37 give us a hint of something special. These verses tell us that judging the voice of God requires a level of spiritual maturity. Some believe that only prophets can judge prophecy. But, verse 37 discredits that idea. The mere fact that Paul is evoking the aid of the spiritual person alongside the prophet tells us they are counterbalances. If Paul thought it was wise to call for the gifting of both, who are we to disagree. Either way, someone needs to judge what we prophesy. I will say more about this subject in #7.

Exercise self-control. It is essential that you embrace this principle, as well. Sometimes prophecy gets a bad rap simply because of the erratic behavior of those prophesying. One fear that many pastors have centers around this fact. A lot of pastors can attest to the fact that untrained prophetic people will often crop up in their churches and create confusion. How do they create confusion? Well, by running around the church prophesying to everyone. To a gift like a pastor whose function promotes order, this is extremely irritating.

New prophets sometimes lack the understanding that the gift is subject to their control. Often, they cite Jeremiah's words, *"His fire was shut up in my bones, and I could not hold it back."* That is how they justify their behavior.

I once saw a young lady take over the microphone during a worship service and speak a word. At the time, the service was in a high time of praise. Seeing the opportunity, she took the microphone. This action alone was not a problem. It became problematic when the senior officiant tried to recover the microphone. Though he was in charge of the service, she would not give the mic back to him. Her actions were out of order. Also, as you can imagine, it made for quite the spectacle. But why didn't she wait? Well, it was burning in her heart, and she could not hold it back. Is that the right answer? No! 1 Corinthians 14:32 tells us that the spirit of the prophet is subject to the prophet. What does that mean? It means that the prophet has control over what he or she hears. Why would God give us control over this gift? Well, one, to avoid confusion. Second, to allow us to write it down so that it can be judged. If this young lady had submitted it for judging maybe the whole thing would have gone differently. Either way, we must operate with order. That does not happen without self-control!

Yield to the revelation of others (take turns). Amos 3:7 teaches us that God does not give everything to one person. Though some think of themselves as possessing all knowledge, he or she does not. For that reason, we must learn how to hear each other and take turns speaking. Paul tells us. *"... and if anything is revealed, let the first be quiet."*

There is nothing worse than a know-it-all. I know. I was one of them. In my early years, I thought that I knew everything there was to know about God. I was arrogant and often spoke over others. I did not hesitate to share my insight with all the perceived puny minds in my presence. I was good at talking and terrible at listening. Then I was humbled when I ran into people who were just as gifted as me. I learned at that moment that I was one of many in God's complex network of informers. I was different but not indispensable.

1 Corinthians 13:9 says:

"We know in part; therefore, we prophesy in part."

Notice that word "part." It means that everyone gets only a slither of God's infinite knowledge. It is the concept behind the idea of God's body. Paul tells us that we are only a "part" of the body. He further emphasizes that "part" means that we have a role. Roles communicate that we have limitations. I don't care how gifted a prophet may be; he is limited. He can only prophesy with limited vision. Therefore, God gives us others to provide another point of view. Look at what Paul says in verse 14:29.

If anything is revealed to another (speaking of the two or three appointed to prophesy that day), who sits by let the first keep silent."

In other words, God only gives you so much, and then you must hear the rest from another.

Say something meaningful! Prophecy was never meant to be vague ramblings. The communication gifts worked together in the early church to provide doctrine. Most of us think of the gifts as separated into three categories; Revelation gifts *(word of wisdom, knowledge, and discerning of spirits)*: Speaking gifts *(prophecy, tongues, and interpretation of tongues)*: Power gifts *(gifts of healings, faith, and working of miracles)*. But, when you take a close look at this listing, there are only two categories: communication gifts which include both the revelation and speaking gifts, and power gifts, which include those gifts that forcefully do something. 1 Corinthians 14 is about the communication gifts.

The communication gifts in biblical times were used to provide doctrine for the newly developing church. It is this understanding that provides the basis for the belief that these gifts are no longer necessary. For that reason, I covered the three stages of revelation. The communication gifts, though foundational in developing doctrine, were not foundational in revelation. God did not use these gifts at the level of Abraham, Moses, or Jesus. These gifts were used in much the same way that God gave revelation to Peter and Paul. That means that prophecy was part of a system of divine communication that allowed for learning. You may question how this is true.

Look at 1 Corinthians 14. Paul's entire argument regarding the use of tongues in the church was about learning. He said:

> Pursue love, and desire spiritual gifts, but especially that you may prophesy. For he who speaks in a tongue does not speak to men but to God, for no one **understands** him; however, in the spirit he speaks mysteries. But he who prophesies speaks edification and exhortation and comfort to men. He who speaks in a tongue edifies himself, but he who prophesies **edifies the church**. I wish you all spoke with tongues, but even more that you prophesied; for he who prophesies is greater than he who speaks with tongues, **unless indeed he interprets, that the church may receive edification.**

Notice the keywords in the verses, "understand" and "edifies." How is prophecy edifying to the church? Paul tells us in verse 18.

> I thank my God I speak with tongues more than you all; yet in the church I would rather speak five words with my understanding, **that I may teach** others also, than ten thousand words in a tongue.

Verses 29-31 take is a step further. They read:

Let two or three prophets speak, and let the others judge. But if anything is revealed to one that sits by, let the first keep silent. For you can all prophesy one by one, ***that all may learn*** *and all may be encouraged.*

Do you see that Paul equates prophecy to a vehicle of learning? Today we have a shallow view of prophecy. A lot of people prophesying seek to share on the fringes of the gift. They prefer to say things like, "God is going to take us into a new era" or "God is going to give us a great revival." But, look at the insight Paul gives us into the gift of prophecy. In 1 Corinthians 13:2, he writes about the gift using these words.

And though I have the gift of prophecy, ***and understand all mysteries and all knowledge...***

Paul was teaching us that prophecy is a vehicle of revelation whereby we can learn from God Himself. This truth tells us that prophecy should be meaningful. That is not to say that the way that we do it now is wrong. Nonetheless, there is a deeper flow of wisdom in the mind of God than what we are accustomed to hearing. Likewise, I suspect that the opposers to prophecy agree. I don't think that they hate prophecy as much as they hate not seeing anything substantial come from hearing from God. I struggle with this myself. I often struggle to understand how people can hear from God and be bound, depressed, suicidal, broke, clueless, without purpose, and more.

How is it that God's voice has not produced a better version of you? I talk to God a lot. Most people appreciate the level of insight I have into various subjects. Likewise, most people agree that I am hearing from someone way smarter than us all. The source of my wisdom is either God or the devil, but it is not coming from me. That being said, I have never had a conversation with God that did not result in the betterment of my person. I am more educated because of His voice. I am more knowledgeable about spiritual matters; better as a husband and father, more able to live righteously and victoriously, more purpose-driven, more focused, and wealthier.

Moreover, it is all the result of hearing the voice of God. So how is it that people who say that they listen to the voice of God are child molesters, drunks, thieves, whores (male and females), and adulterers? How is it that God's voice has not produced victory in the life of the hearer? Even as we look through scripture, the most common result of hearing the voice of God was victory. He said to Jeremiah in chapter 23:9:

"My word is like a hammer that breaks rocks into pieces."

Again, He says in Jeremiah 23:22:

"If they had stood in My counsel and spoken a word from Me the people would have repented."

Is God Still Speaking?

Finally, He says to Isaiah in chapter 55:11:

"My word will prosper where I send it."

All of this means one thing; whenever God speaks, He says something meaningful." I suspect that following His example might make it easier for the naysayers to embrace the reality that God still speaks.

Seeing prophecy as something we learn from may be a bit of an abstract concept. Therefore, here is an example. In the summer of 2018, I was invited to speak at a pastor's anniversary. Upon receiving the invitation, I asked God what He wanted me to say. Over time He responded with a vision of my fire logo. It was clear that He wanted to talk about fire. As I listened, He brought up Acts 2, the moment when the fire of the Holy Ghost fell on the disciples. Over the next few days, I read the passage allowing the Holy Spirit to unpack its truth. A couple of weeks before the engagement, He spoke to me in prayer. He showed me that there were a certain number of preachers that would be present. He also informed me that they had been meeting to discuss how they could reach their communities. He said that they were frustrated and a few of them were planning to quit the ministry. I even heard them praying for an answer. With that basic information, God tailored the sermon just for them. He told me to preach from the idea "When the Fire Comes." The sermon was about how the Holy Spirit gave the church the ability to reach the world by giving them the languages of the world. The application of the message was precise. If they wanted to reach the world, then they would have to depend on God to give them unique strategies that were not native to their understanding but would be recognizable to the audience. So, I got up that day and preached the message the Lord gave me. At the conclusion, I called them up and told them what God showed me about their frustration. I then prayed for them. When the service ended, a preacher approached me. He said, "What you said is true. The other pastors and I have been meeting. We are trying to figure out how to reach these people." The word of the Lord was accurate. It was prophetic, and it was meaningful. It was predictive, yet full of useful information that helped them to see a way forward. In fact, the prophetic word was an answer to their prayer. I suspect that meaningful prophecy is the preference. I think people are saying, "If God is going to speak to us, then we want it to be meaningful."

#6 Defer to Scripture

I have already proven that the written word of God is the voice of God. Now I want to focus on the idea that God is consistent. That means that we can always defer to scripture. Often, prophets think of themselves as possessing unique revelation—unique meaning that they believe that God has spoken something to them that nobody has ever heard before. More often than not, they are wrong. I recall traveling across the country to see a man that made such a claim. It was the first time that I spent $700 on anything. To my surprise, his big revelation was something that God spoke to me days earlier.

From the experience, I learned that no one has an exclusive seat at God's table. In fact, Amos 3:7 tells us that God reveals His secrets to His servants, not His servant. This passage fortifies the idea that God establishes an idea by the witness of more than one vessel. It further teaches us that consistency is a part of the nature of God. Therefore, when prophesying, our words should not be so far out of God's character that we cannot find anything similar in His word.

Have you ever thought about the fact that the Bible is harmonious from cover to cover? Has it ever occurred to you that though it has many authors, who wrote over many centuries, that it is consistent? For instance, God spoke about Jesus in Genesis 3. He talked about Him in Isaiah. He spoke of Him in the book of Revelation. Look at the span of time covered. Yet, no author contradicts the other authors regarding the matter of the Christ. Even the apocalyptic books are consistent in what they describe for the future. Again, this tells us that God is consistent in His messaging.

Most of the time, when prophecy or prophetic doctrine goes wrong, it violates this principle. Every false Christian cult such as the Mormons is an example of such. We know that Joseph Smith was in error because He heard something no one else had heard. We know that David Koresh was wrong; because he heard something else no one else had heard. Their doctrines reflected the uniqueness of an idea. So unique, in fact, that God had not told even the biblical authors.

This takes us back to the building principle "here a little, there a little, line upon line, precept upon precept." Whenever I hear a so-called revelation that fails to build upon the foundation of what came before it, I conclude that it is error. God, who is progressively unveiled, would not give us something new that invalidates what He said before. Deferring to scripture protects us from deception.

#7 Encourage Accountability

As mentioned in a previous chapter, some fear using the phrase, "God said" and "Thus says the Lord." Their apprehension comes from the fear that those receiving prophetic ministry lack the ability to challenge the validity of a prophetic word. Some people irreverently confuse prophets as gods. That being the case, they accept every word from them as perfect. What a grave error! We can never assume that a person has 100 percent prophetic accuracy. Even though I wrote what some call the most comprehensive book on the subject of hearing God's voice, I still get it wrong from time to time. That simply proves that I am human. Likewise, so are your brothers and sisters in Christ. No one is perfect in serving the purpose of God.

I cannot stress enough the need to embrace our humanity. Doing so allows us to create an atmosphere conducive to safe prophetic practices. It also promotes an environment of growth. It is easy to learn how to hear God correctly when doing so in a place that is free from condemnation and supports learning. Still, you should know that It is impossible to learn without failing. Furthermore, failing leads to positive discovery. That, folks, is the truth about growing in the prophetic.

Even the biblical prophets allowed their ministries to develop in an educational and mentoring environment. Look at 2 Kings 2:1-17. Elisha, following Elijah, crossed paths with several persons described as "the sons of the prophets." These persons were students of older prophetic men. Elisha was also a servant to Elijah for three years before Elijah's ascent to heaven. God called Elisha in 1 King's 19 when He told downtrodden Elijah to anoint him as his replacement. When we read about his incredible prophetic ministry, we gawk in awe, but forget about his training. The sons of the prophets were learning the craft. They were learning how to see, hear, and interpret their experiences with God. After all, the consequences for error, according to Deuteronomy 13 and 18, was death. I am sure that motivated them to pay attention in class.

To the prophet reading this, it is okay to miss it. To the pastor desiring to start a prophetic ministry in his or her church, it is okay if the prophet gets it wrong from time to time. As I stated in #1, try education, not eradication! We must allow and encourage people to try to hear from God and grow in their giftings and callings.

Test the Words

Paul's profound words to the Corinthians confirms that it is possible to "prophe-lie." Again, in his letter, he encouraged them to *"let the others, judge."* These words convey the reality of deception and error. Why else would Paul write such words except that the threat was valid? The first step to creating an atmosphere for the voice of God is acknowledging the possibility of error. This truth applies to both the prophet and the recipient.

No one should feel cornered by the words, "God said." The Bible does not teach blind submission to those words. In fact, Paul wrote these words about prophecy.

> *"Do not despise prophecy. Test all things; hold fast to what is good." (1 Thess. 5:20-21, NKJV)"*

Look at the apostle's advice for dealing with prophecy. He tells us to "test" it. That means that we must put in place a system of accountability. While it is okay to miss God from time to time, it is not cool to dismiss the problem. Accountability is important. That's why I started with getting us to embrace our broken nature. If we can acknowledge our deficiencies, testing our words will prove our humility. It also allows us to submit ourselves to scrutiny willingly.

Advice for the Prophet

Allow recipients of prophetic ministry to disagree with you. It is okay if they do not accept your words. Sometimes we get it wrong. Other times, God causes the recipient to understand it later. The truth is that only God can confirm and establish His word in a person's heart. I once prophesied a word that did not come to pass until twenty years later. At the time I gave it, the person was nowhere near ready to receive it. It is not our responsibility to prove our ministries. God will do that Himself. Sometimes we feel as though the rejection of a prophecy kills its futuristic power. That is not so.

2 King 7 records the story of a man who questioned the validity of Elisha's prophetic words. His doubt did not prevent God from doing what He intended to do. The same truth applies to Israel's descent into captivity. They rejected Jeremiah's words. On one occasion, a man assaulted him. He was even cast into a prison cell because of his unfavorable prophecies. Neither situation stopped his predictions from manifesting. It all happens in God's time. Still, as prophetic people, we must be mature enough to distinguish between the rejection of our words and the rejection of our person. Deliver your word. Do so with power and boldness. Next, allow others to judge it. Give them room to disagree with you, and do not take it personally. Finally, let God prove His words right.

Advice for the Recipient

Prophets are not gods! Instead, they are His representatives. They are human even though they may show forth extreme levels of giftedness. Their humanity also means that they are prone to error and fallacy. As we consider Paul's words in 1 Thessalonians 5:20-21 and I Corinthians 14:29, know that you have every right to disagree with an untested word. Especially if it comes from someone you either do not know or whose ministry is unfamiliar to you. Do not allow the word's "Thus says the Lord" to intimidate you. Test "everything" hold fast to what is "true!"

When testing a prophetic word, here are some things that you can do to aid the growth of both you and the prophet.

Provide honest feedback. If the prophet gives a word that you do not agree with or understand, let him or her know. Please do so in a compassionate way. It can be awkward to be wrong, especially if a crowd is present. Remember, it takes a fair amount of bravery to prophesy. This is especially true in today's church culture.

Positive feedback allows the prophet to recalibrate. Sometimes the word is right, but the prophet's interpretation of what is heard or seen is off. This is called presumption. It occurs when the prophet fails to ask God the question, "What does this mean?" Sometimes we unfortunately impose meaning.

For example, once, as I was prophesying over a woman, I saw an image of King Kong beating his chest. I immediately assumed that God was showing me the woman's pride. As I kept watching the vision, I saw the ape put a little sailboat on the sea. Over the years, I have come to understand vessels to symbolize ministry. I'm glad I did not tell her the first thing I saw. The image was not about her pride; it was about the frustration she felt and the rejection she experienced in her church. It was about a ministry struggling to set sail. Can you imagine the damage I would have done by jumping to a conclusion about the vision? Sometimes prophetic people move too quickly. God calls that presumption. And, sometimes prophets get it wrong. Either way, honest and thoughtful feedback allows them to improve upon their ability to serve the Body of Christ.

Record the word. God often told prophets to record their words. Habakkuk 2 and John's Book of Revelation are great examples. Recording the word takes the urgency out of the situation. It relieves the pressure and sense to immediately comply with what is heard. Also, it makes the word available for testing.

Empower yourself with knowledge. We have all heard or read Hosea 4:6, "My people perish for lack of knowledge." It is true. Many people impacted by immature or malicious prophetic ministry don't know how to discern God's voice. Not only do they not know how to recognize His voice, but there is also often little evidence of their efforts to learn how to do so. Few things irritate me more than saints who try to ride the coattails of those who paid the price to walk intimately with God. The same relationship we have with God is available to all. But it requires consistent study, prayer, and a willingness to learn God's word as well as His ways. As stated earlier, learning means developing the patience to stay the course through failure and ups and downs.

Here is something that will encourage your pursuit of God. James 4:8 tells us to draw near to God, and He will draw near to us. Notice the order put forth. Often we sing songs and make prayers, asking God to bring us near to Himself. However, the Bible declares that it is our pursuit of Him that causes Him to pursue us. The bottom line is, you must want to be closer to God. Then you need to take the necessary steps to satisfy that fire in you. If you do, discerning the word of the Lord through a prophet will be much easier.

#8 Put Prophecy in Its Proper Place

Prophecy is a sign, not a guide. Oftentimes, it is allowed to lead where it should follow. However, Jesus said this to the disciples before He left earth.

> *And these signs will follow those who believe: In My name, they will cast out demons; they will speak with new tongues; (Mark 16:17, NKJV)*

Now look at the order of events in this passage.

> *So then, after the Lord had spoken to them, He was received up into heaven, and sat down at the right hand of God. And they went out and preached everywhere, the Lord working with them and confirming the word through the accompanying signs. Amen.*

The signs did not come before the word. I know what you are thinking. You are saying to yourself, "Wait, prophecy is not a sign and wonder. It is a gift of the Holy Spirit. Isn't it?" Yes, prophecy is a gift of the Holy Spirit. It, along with all the other gifts mentioned in 1 Corinthians 12, are signs also.

What is the function of a sign? A sign has two goals. One, to inform you and two, to guide your focus and movement. Signs let you know that you are going in the right or wrong direction. They keep you on track and identify the pathway forward. Can you imagine crossing paths with a blank sign? As a graphic designer, I know how important and powerful a sign communicates. If worded wrong and pointed in the wrong direction, a sign can cause quite a bit of confusion. In my opinion, that is what we have happening today. Some people are turned off by the prophetic simply because the sign is either blank or pointed in no specific direction. Today, people treat prophecy like some type of heavenly heroin for pain.

At one point, I belonged to a few prophetic groups on social media. They advertised themselves as a safe place for wounded prophetic voices to exercise their gifting. They also offered training to those new to the gift. For the most part, it was a good experience. I am always proud to see believers trying to grow, even if they have to use unconventional ways to do so.

Nonetheless, there was one thing I noticed in these groups. In every one, there were many people living by prophecy. It was nothing to see a person post a request for a prophetic word simply because they did not feel happy at the moment. It would only take seconds for their social media feed to fill with words of hope and inspiration, in the name of the Lord. What irritated me about this behavior is the fact that it was common to see the same names surfacing daily. Each time they wanted a new word. Could God really want to speak to the same person every single day via prophecy? It was clear to me that a lot of them were following the sign, instead of it following them. I was not alone in my disdain for this practice. The leaders of the group also noted the same thing. Eventually, they discouraged this behavior and encouraged those seeking God to do two things; One, seek God for yourself. And two, seek God in His word.

It is easy for me to see how such imbalance can turn away curious believers from prophecy. Not to mention the other practices such as those who announce a specific date for Jesus' return. History is full of such examples and the tremendous loss incurred by those following the sign. How do we get around this type of error? Simple, put prophecy into its proper context.

How is Prophecy a Sign?

> *"If there arises among you a prophet or a dreamer of dreams, and he gives you **a sign or a wonder**, and the sign or the wonder comes to pass, of which he spoke to you, saying, 'Let us go after other gods'—which you have not known—'and let us serve them,' you shall not listen to the words of that prophet or that dreamer of dreams, for the Lord your God is testing you to know whether you love the Lord your God with all your heart and with all your soul.*

Look at what God calls prophecy. He calls it a "sign" or a "wonder" in two places in the text. I also want to point to the role of the sign or the wonder in this passage. It and the wonder are attached to the message, which are noted as being distinctly separate from the sign. Its purpose is to validate the message. Remember, a sign has two goals, communicating and directing. Here we see the message and the act of directing a person's attention to or away from God.

Are there any examples of this truth? Sure, there are plenty. Let's look at a few of them. God sent Moses to Pharaoh with a message saying, "Let My people go!" To reinforce the message, God gave His servant 12 signs, which are also called plagues. The message itself was akin to a short sermonette. Still, God knew that Pharaoh and Israel would need more than words. So, He gave them something to guide their focus to Himself. Moses' life was full of prophetic signs.

Though I can rattle off many examples, I will only share one more. Look at 1 Samuel 10:1-9. It reads.

Then Samuel took a flask of oil and poured it on his head, and kissed him and said: "Is it not because the Lord has anointed you commander over His inheritance? When you have departed from me today, you will find two men by Rachel's tomb in the territory of Benjamin at Zelzah; and they will say to you, 'The donkeys which you went to look for have been found. And now your father has ceased caring about the donkeys and is worrying about you, saying, "What shall I do about my son?"' Then you shall go on forward from there and come to the terebinth tree of Tabor. There three men going up to God at Bethel will meet you, one carrying three young goats, another carrying three loaves of bread, and another carrying a skin of *wine. And they will greet you and give you two loaves of bread, which you shall receive from their hands. After that you shall come to the hill of God where the Philistine garrison is. And it will happen, when you have come there to the city, that you will meet a group of prophets coming down from the high place with a stringed instrument, a tambourine, a flute, and a harp before them; and they will be prophesying. Then the Spirit of the Lord will come upon you, and you will prophesy with them and be turned into another man. And let it be, **when these signs come to you,** that you do as the occasion demands; for God is with you. You shall go down before me to Gilgal; and surely I will come down to you to offer burnt offerings and make sacrifices of peace offerings. Seven days you shall wait, till I come to you and show you what you should do."*

Read what it says next:

*So it was, when he had turned his back to go from Samuel, that God gave him another heart; **and all those signs** came to pass that day.*

Do you see it yet? While the prophetic gift provided guidance, the manifestation provided focus. God's message to the newly anointed king was God's primary concern. The prophetic unveiling of future events was merely a bonus.

The Other Side of The Coin

While some are following the signs, others are operating without one. It is tremendously frustrating to watch preachers share the Good News of Jesus with no resulting fruit. Every Sunday, many altars never see new converts. Might the problem be the missing signage? As we know, there are multitudes of religions in the world. Likewise, the majority of them are good-natured, as evidenced by their followers. Just consider the eastern religions. Asians are some of the most productive and peaceful people on the planet. It is easy to see why they are grounded in their faith. But, we know that they do not have the truth regarding salvation. The question is: what makes our often chaotic and divided Christian community, right? Is it the Bible? Is it something we just know? How do we gauge our faith?

Many American churches use what is called The Romans Road, in their proselyting. If you are familiar with this process, it presents the Gospel message using only the book of Romans. It is an excellent tool for new and seasoned believers alike. It is simple, orderly, and understandable. However, it relies on the Bible as the sole source of soul winning. Those promoting this technique tell you to allow the Holy Spirit to work through the word. To their credit, He often does. For that reason, I still consider it an effective evangelistic technique.

Nonetheless, many times, the evangelized person argues with the scriptures. Likewise, those sharing the scriptures often become frustrated with the person's perceived disrespect

Addressing Our Fear of Deception

for the Bible. They say, "How can you argue with God's word?" To the person hearing that statement, they respond, "How do you know it is God's word?" While this is offensive to the believer, it is a fair question. Every major religion and even Christian cults have a book that they claim is true and divine. Why should they believe our version of the truth, just based on the belief that it is in the Bible?

Not only do we encounter opposition to the Bible during moments of evangelism, but we also experience rivalry in our routine settings. How many arguments about scripture take place in the office? What about at the family reunion? Or, sometimes they happen while traveling. This same thing happened to me.

I was flying out to California to see Morris Cerullo. It was my first time flying as an adult. To help myself settle in, I brought a few books. One of them was a book on prayer. As we prepared for takeoff, an older gentleman sitting next to me glanced over and noticed my book. Without hesitation, he immediately attacked my faith. He said there was no God. Religion starts wars and messes up the world. He just went on and on and on. My flight was from Washington, D.C. to San Diego, California. Overall, it would take eight hours to reach my destination. Fortunately, we had a layover. Still, I spent several hours trying to convince him of the existence of God and the saving power of Jesus. I was not successful in the latter, but I was able to move him from his atheist stoop.

This guy did not care about my scriptures. He had complaints, and he wanted them addressed. That being the case,

I had to turn to my bestie the Holy Spirit to guide the conversation. It was my access to His incredible knowledge and wisdom, obtained through spiritual gifts, that allowed me to move this man from being an angry atheist to a calm, smiling God-seeker. At the core of this man's argument was the question, "Where is God when you need Him.? That is what people really want to know. They do not want us to hurl scriptures at them. They want to see the God of the scriptures in action.

Some believe it is evil to seek a sign. After all, that is what Jesus said. Still, Jesus also told many people to believe the signs when they didn't trust His words. When asked by John the Baptist, whether or not He was the Christ, He told John to look at the signs. He used the miracles as proof of His word. Not only did He tell this to John. He also demonstrated it to His disciples upon ascending to heaven. Mark 16:20:21 reads:

> *So then, after the Lord had spoken to them, He was received up into heaven, and sat down at the right hand of God. And they went out and preached everywhere, the Lord working with them and confirming the word through the accompanying signs. Amen.*

Jesus was not condemning signs as evil. He was communicating to them the abomination of seeking proof despite the obvious. The Jews wanted a man doing miracles to out due the miracles He was already doing.

While I do not advocate that we follow signs, I definitely support them following us. Deuteronomy also confirms this idea. The sign God speaks of in chapter thirteen was to validate the vessel as much as it did the message. That is what Jesus did in Mark 16. One of the reasons we trust in the apostles as foundations to the faith is God's evident hand on their lives. In fact, most theologians hold fast to the idea that the miracles were specific to their ministry for the sole purpose of confirming their apostolic callings. I agree with this in part. I, too, believe the works established their ministries. Not only theirs, but ours as well. For that reason, this book is dedicated to helping believers embrace both the message and the sign. If we fail to acknowledge God's right to say who He supports, we leave ourselves open to false teachers.

No, we are not to follow signs. Yes, they should follow us. Finally, if we allow prophecy to do what God designed it to do, we will see greater success in the end. No one can prove the existence of God or establish Jesus as the Messiah, better than the Holy Spirit. He can easily do what we find frustrating to accomplish.

These Eight Words of Wisdom

These eight simple, yet profound words of wisdom can help us embrace God's prophetic voice in the Church. I know it has been rough thus far. Some have endured confusion, pain, misdirection, and even excommunication because of immature and rouge prophetic practices. I get it. There are legitimate reasons to be resistant to the words, "Thus says the Lord." Nonetheless, I must say as a witness, that the benefits of doing prophetic ministry right far outweigh the risk. Give God a chance to show the joys of genuine prophetic ministry.

Finally, let's review these eight principles. As we learn them, they will assist us in implementing God's voice safely into the fabric of our lives. They are: #1 Try education not eradication, #2 Learn to discern, #3 Find a balance, #4 Be realistic, #5 Practice precaution, #6 Defer to scripture, #7 Encourage accountability, and #8 Put prophecy into its proper place.

7
Chapter

Addressing a Specific Fear

Psychics and Prophets

This chapter could reasonably be considered an extension of the last. Much like the previous chapter, it also addresses the subject of fear. Though, this chapter deals with a particular fear, one that needs to be treated separately. Let's talk about psychics and how they differ from prophets.

Many things keep the Church at bay when it comes to embracing modern-day prophecy. One thing that hinders the acceptance of this gift is the fear of occultic infiltration in the form of psychic activity. Many people even wonder whether psychics and prophets are the same. Some believe that the two are the same. Others subscribe to the idea that psychics are lost prophets using their gifting for Satan. Some people even believe that psychics are demon-possessed individuals.

Finally, there are those convinced that psychics are con artists with a knack for manipulating people's minds. Which is right? More importantly, how do we reconcile what we know about prophetic ministry and psychic expression, and why do we need to address this matter?

The answer to the last question is simple; we must address this matter so that we can discern the differences between these two expressions. Furthermore, we also need real prophets to know how distinctly different they are from the counterfeit prophetic ministry. To do that, we must make ourselves knowledgeable about the differences between the two. I learned many years ago that one of the most dangerous persons is an ignorant one. Likewise, nothing inspires fear more than the lack of truthful information. For that reason, I want to look at the differences between psychics and prophets. To make the distinction between the two, I want to examine the following:

- Different Sources
- Different Operations

Different Sources

Sometimes believers forget that our adversary is a supernatural being. The Bible informs us that this evil entity has power. The Bible, much to my displeasure, also refers to him as the "god" of this age" (See 2 Cor. 4:4). Not only does the apostle Paul call him a god, but the scriptures also depict his power.

Addressing a Specific Fear

Finally, the Bible shares with us that he can invest that power in a human host. Let's look at a few examples. Exodus 7:8-13 first introduces us to Satan's invested power.

> *The Lord said to Moses and Aaron, "When Pharaoh says to you, 'Perform a miracle,' then say to Aaron, 'Take your staff and throw it down before Pharaoh,' and it will become a snake." So Moses and Aaron went to Pharaoh and did just as the Lord commanded. Aaron threw his staff down in front of Pharaoh and his officials, and it became a snake. Pharaoh then summoned wise men and sorcerers, and the Egyptian magicians also did the same things by their secret arts: Each one threw down his staff and it became a snake. But Aaron's staff swallowed up their staffs. Yet Pharaoh's heart became hard and he would not listen to them, just as the Lord had said.*

Take notice of the magicians' abilities. By Satan's power, they were able to replicate Moses' miracles. Also, keep in mind that they did not perform cheap parlor tricks. In their first challenge to Moses, these demonically empowered men brought an inanimate object to life. Their next two tricks were equally impressive. They turned water to blood, which demonstrated their ability to manipulate the properties of matter. Then they called frogs onto the land, demonstrating the ability to control various aspects of nature. These instances are clear examples of Satan's power.

Here is another example of Satan's ability to empower human beings. It is found in Act 16:16-19 (NIV). This story relates precisely to our topic.

> *Once when we were going to the place of prayer, we were met by a female slave who had a spirit by which she predicted the future. She earned a great deal of money for her owners by fortune-telling. She followed Paul and the rest of us, shouting, "These men are servants of the Most High God, who are telling you the way to be saved." She kept this up for many days. Finally Paul became so annoyed that he turned around and said to the spirit, "In the name of Jesus Christ I command you to come out of her!" At that moment the spirit left her. When her owners realized that their hope of making money was gone, they seized Paul and Silas and dragged them into the marketplace to face the authorities.*

Please note that the young girl possessed foretelling ability. Likewise, it tells us that a demonic influence fueled her power. The passage plainly tells us this much by stating that she had a spirit. The New King James Version says it another way. It tells us that she was *"possessed"* with a spirit of divination. The spirit or demon of divination is a psychic spirit. The Old Testament uses the term "familiar spirit."

When reading about this girl, you may wonder, as I did, "Were her predictions accurate?" To answer that question, I want you to consider one key factor. The passage says that she

Addressing a Specific Fear

earned her masters a great deal of money. Now, ask yourself this question; How many people do you know continuously utilizing the services of an inefficient person? Her lucrative success is evidence of her proficiency. This essential piece of information tells us that psychics can access supernatural knowledge. The question is which spirit is the origin of that information.

There are other examples. I will show you two more. The first comes from the book of 1 Samuel. 1 Samuel 18:10 reads.

And it happened on the next day that the distressing spirit from God came upon Saul, and he prophesied inside the house. So David played music with his hand, as at other times; but there was a spear in Saul's hand.

Now read 1 Samuel 19:22-24. It reads.

Then he also went to Ramah, and came to the great well that is at Sechu. So he asked, and said, "Where are Samuel and David?" And someone said, "Indeed they are at Naioth in Ramah." So he went there to Naioth in Ramah. Then the Spirit of God was upon him also, and he went on and prophesied until he came to Naioth in Ramah. And he also stripped off his clothes and prophesied before Samuel in like manner, and lay down naked all that day and all that night. Therefore they say, "Is Saul also among the prophets?"

Both passages speak of Saul prophesying. They also show us two different sources behind his prophetic expression. When researching both, I discovered that the use of the word "prophesied" in both passages had the same Hebrew word. That tells us that the expression was the same, though the sources were not.

Now let's look at the last example. This time it comes from the life of the apostle Peter. Read Matthew 16. In this chapter, Jesus commends Peter and affirms his ability to hear the voice of God. It reads:

Jesus answered and said to him, "Blessed are you, Simon Bar-Jonah, for flesh and blood has not revealed this to you, but My Father who is in heaven.

Then the unthinkable happens. Read verses 22-23.

Then Peter took Him aside and began to rebuke Him, saying, "Far be it from You, Lord; this shall not happen to You!" But He turned and said to Peter, "Get behind Me, Satan! You are an offense to Me, for you are not mindful of the things of God, but the things of men."

In the first part of the chapter, Peter heard God's voice and communicated what he heard. Then, just a few short verses later, he listened to Satan's voice and again, delivered what he heard. This time, instead of commending him, Jesus rebuked Him for listening to the wrong voice. Still, we see two sources of spiritual communication.

This lesson was a very significant one for Peter. He needed to know how to discern between the voices of these two spirits. "Why," you may ask? Well, who preached the first prophetic sermon in the New Testament? Peter did. Likewise, Acts shows Peter repeatedly filled with the divine inspiration of God throughout his life. Each time resulted in a vocal expression. For that reason, and because of His great foreknowledge about Peter, Jesus did what was necessary to ensure that Peter understood the importance of recognizing God's voice so that he was not a pawn in Satan's game. Remember, this was the same Peter that Jesus prayed for because Satan had requested permission to sift him as wheat (See Luke 22:31-34). Try to imagine that day and its repercussions had Peter spoke by the wrong spirit.

Overall, his example, as well as the others, teaches us that there are two sources of spiritual communication. Psychics obviously yield themselves to the less favorable one.

Different Operations

To the untrained and uninformed person, revelatory ability defines the prophetic ministry. For example, when speaking to a Samaritan woman at a well, Jesus revealed her marital status by unique insight. His actions led the woman to conclude that He was a prophet. His example confirms that the prophetic ministry is indeed revelatory. This story also verifies people's expectations about prophetic people as revelatory ministers. However, Jesus was not a prophet because He had special insight. Yes, He was revelatory, but He was so much more. It is those differences, some of which I address later, that solidified His calling to be a prophetic voice.

While prophets are undoubtedly gifted with unique insight, this is only part of what makes a prophet prophetic. Psychics are also revelatory. For this reason, we often confuse these two expressions as being the same. Though prophets and psychics are similar in appearance, they do not have the same end goal in mind. Yes, both gifts are capable of revealing the secrets of a person's past and present; Yes, they can also foretell future events. Yet, as impressive as these abilities may be, none of them should be considered benchmarks for identifying genuine prophetic ministry. If they were the defining standards, then psychics are prophets too. We know, however, that this is not true.

If prophets and psychics are the same operationally, how are they different? To get to the bottom of this, we must start by understanding the term revelation and its various levels.

Defining the Term Revelation

What is revelation? We have been talking about it the whole book, but what is it? The word revelation means to unveil or uncover. It can simply be defined as God turning on the lights and allowing us to see what is present. When we hear the word revelation, we often think of hearing or seeing something new. However, the appropriate way to think about this word is to associate it with the uncovering of something hid-

Addressing a Specific Fear

den from our sight. That is an essential piece of information. Some fear that acknowledging prophetic insight is an admission that God is adding something new to us. But the truth is, prophets don't hear or see anything new. They merely show us what is already present or planned.

If we read Matthew 16:13-21 again, we see a great example of revelation. In this chapter of Mark, Jesus asked the disciples a question. He asked, *"Who do men say that I am?"* After rattling off a few prominent names, Peter said, *"You are the Christ, the Son of the living God."* Then Jesus said, *"Flesh and blood did not reveal this to you but My Father which is in heaven."* Peter did not see anything new. Jesus had healed many people by this time. He had also walked on water and multiplied bread. He did not suddenly become divine. He was always God, and the Father allowed Peter to see the truth that had always been present.

Revelation always shows us what God sees and knows. Furthermore, there are three things you need to know about revelation to be able to discern the difference between genuine prophetic ministry and psychic expression. They are:

1. Revelation can show us events in time
2. Revelation can show us what's in God's mind to do
3. Revelation can show us what's in God's heart to do

A lot of people are not aware of these three types of revelations. Actually, I prefer to see them as levels of revelations. You will understand that statement as I unpack each one.

Revelations of Events in Time

There is no doubt that God is all-knowing. His omniscient nature is the bedrock of our ability to trust Him. There are few things more frightening than being lost with no way to get back on course. Well, we don't even need to worry about that with God. He knows everything there is to know. Thank You, Jesus! Knowing that He knows what is going to happen next assures us that we can blindly follow Him wherever He takes us.

Because God knows all things, He also chooses to share some of that knowledge with various people. More specifically, He shows us specific events in the future. Here are some examples.

Joseph's interpretation of Pharaoh's dream revealed a prediction about a famine (See Genesis 41:1-36). The prophet Samuel predicted the events of Saul's day (See 1 Samuel 10:1-13). Elisha also predicted the reemergence of the Israeli economy (See 2 Kings 7:1-20). Finally, Agabus predicted an earthquake and Paul's imprisonment (See Acts 11:28 and 21:10-11). Each of these illustrates God's ability to give people knowledge about future events.

This predictive characteristic intrigue a lot of people and often spurs an interest in prophetic ministry. Sometimes that interest is unhealthy. It can even lead to a fascination with psychics, mediums, and the occult. After all, everyone wants to know what's going to happen in the future.

Predicting the future is part of being prophetic. Though, I must note that it is only a small part. In fact, some prophets

Addressing a Specific Fear

in the Bible never foretold an event. For instance, Adam, Abel, and Abraham never predicted the future. Some prophets, like Noah, only had one insight into the future. Yet, the Bible regards him as a prophet.

Get ready; my next statement may shock you. Predictive revelation, though impressive, is the lowest level of revelation God gives us. By the term "lowest," I say so in comparison to the other two levels of revelation. As mentioned in the last chapter, predictive revelation falls into the category of signs and wonders. A sign, though valuable, is useless without a message. The same is true of predictive revelation. Often, people seek to know the future without also finding the purpose it unveils. Likewise, many prophets define themselves by the ability to produce signs. In their minds, their ministry is fraudulent if they can't tell people about their future. However, this is not true. As I stated before, there are times when prophecy lacks any elements of foreknowledge. By seeking to be espousers of foreknowledge, many prophets have gone off course. Some have even shipwrecked their ministries by succumbing to the pressure to perform for the audience.

During the Covid-19 Pandemic of 2020, many prophets made proclamations of how it would end. To their dismay, many of their prophecies fell to the ground. Why did they fail? They failed because their words were not borne of the Spirit, but from the pressure to provide an answer to the dilemma the world faced. They felt that God had to speak to the situation. And He did. But some prophets added a predictive element to His words because many people associate God with foretelling and not forth-telling. This kind of thinking leads us to speak presumptuously.

That said, prophetic ministry without a doubt requires a lot of discipline. Prophets must learn to be silent when they hear nothing; they must learn to say only what they hear; they must learn prophetic timing for sharing insights. A prophet must also restrain themselves from adding to what could be perceived as a dull or lackluster prophecy.

Moses is such an excellent example of a disciplined prophet. God gave him a simple word, "Let My people go!" What a boring word. Even Pharaoh was unimpressed. Although the word lacked pizzazz, Moses did not predict anything until God gave him something to say.

Yes, predicting the future is an aspect of prophetic ministry. But it is the most insignificant part. There are two other aspects more precious than the ability to foretell the future.

Revelations of God's Mind

Now let's discuss the next level of revelation—the revelation of God's mind. This level of revelation is the second highest. This level, though necessary, does not carry the same value as the revelation of God's heart. In fact, though psychics cannot reach this level, even some prophets never reach the highest level of revelation. Prophets often assume that knowing what is on God's mind equates to understanding what is in His heart. Yet this is not true. In fact, God's heart is not always in agreement with His mind. For instance, look at Ezekiel 22:30.

Addressing a Specific Fear

So I sought for a man among them who would make a wall, and stand in the gap before Me on behalf of the land, that I should not destroy it; but I found no one.

Destroying the offenders was on God's mind. But He clearly did not want to do so. Jonah is another excellent example. We read his story in an earlier chapter. God spent a great deal of time reasoning with the prophet about His heart for the Ninevites. Nevertheless, the prophet could only relate to what was on God's mind, but not what was in His heart. The prophet even confessed that He knew that God would change His mind. That was his reason for running in the first place. His story help us to see the difference between a mental connection and an intimate heart connection with God.

For that reason, I think it is vital to every prophetic ministry to develop an intimate heart to heart relationship with the Holy Spirit. Today, prophetic people seem more interested in entertaining the audience with dazzling words of knowledge than communicating God's heart. I learned years ago that there is a difference between using a gift and ministering that gift. There are people that can sing and, there are people who can minister a song; There are people who can preach, and there are people who can minister a word; Finally, there are those who can prophesy and those who minister the word of the Lord. The most powerful and impactful experience comes through those intimately tied to God's heart.

Kathryn Kuhlman was such an individual. You just knew that she was loved by and in love with God. She did not present her ministry as a show. Instead, she showed the world the power of a partnership with the Holy Spirit. Her every breath seemed to be rooted in an earnest desire to make God's heart leap. Watching her minister reminded me of the disciples in the book of Acts. Today, we treat the gifts of the Holy Spirit as like circus talents. Therefore, it is often hard to see past the minister to see God. This was not so with Kathryn's ministry. It was also not true of the disciples' ministry.

When we read about the disciple named Ananias, we see a man who walked with God and ministered from that relationship. The same is true in Paul's ministry. The early church seemed to understand that we are supposed to be partners with God. They did not see themselves as puppets. Nor did they see the Holy Spirit as merely a resource. We know this by Paul's benediction in 2 Corinthians 13:14, *"The grace of the Lord Jesus Christ, and the love of God, and the communion of the Holy Spirit be with you all. Amen."* Paul was not just God's servant. He was also God's friend. Likewise, God's friend possessed a level of intimate knowledge that others did not. Not him only, but Peter, James, and John also. I suspect that they not only knew what was on God's mind, but they even knew His heart.

The Mind of God

What do I mean by the term "mind of God"? To understand this phrase, we must not only consider that not has feelings, but He also thinks. For instance, Isaiah 55:8-9 tells us that our thoughts are not like His thoughts. Jeremiah 29:11 also

Addressing a Specific Fear

tells us that God knows the thoughts that He thinks about us. Finally, I Corinthians 2:16 tells us that we have the mind of Christ. That is exciting to know, but what does it mean to us? Knowing that He is a thinking being tells us that He is strategic.

Nothing takes God by surprise. Some people believe that He has planned out every event. Others do not subscribe to this type of theology. I am somewhere in the middle. It is evident that God plans. Yet, I also believe that some things happen randomly, and God applies His plans to what He knows about the future. For instance, if you know, before leaving the house that the road you plan to travel is closed due to construction, you would make plans to take an alternate route. That is how I imagine God planning out our lives. The Bible says that Jesus was slain before the foundations of the world. In other words, Jesus died for us before God said, let there be light. Did Jesus really die before time began? No. The passage is a tribute to God's foreknowledge and planning. God did not wait for us to get in trouble to find a remedy. The awesomeness of the passage's truth is that God was willing to kill His only Son for a world that He knew would continue in their evil ways. That, my friends, is true love!

This truth also undergirds the idea that God is a planner. Let's look at a few passages that confirm this idea. The first one comes from Habakkuk 2:2-3.

Then the Lord answered me and said:
"Write the vision and make it plain on tablets,

that he may run who reads it. For the vision is yet for an appointed time; but at the end it will speak, and it will not lie. Though it tarries, wait for it; Because it will surely come, it will not tarry.

Here is another good one. Let's read Amos 3:7.

Surely the Lord God does nothing, unless He reveals His secret to His servants the prophets.

Both passages show us that God plans before He acts. As it relates to our subject, Amos gives us a huge key. He conveys to us that God's plans are secret. Likewise, he tells us that God will not do anything without first revealing those secrets to His servants. Psychics cannot access this level of knowledge. Only "His servants" the prophets can see on this level. That is a major difference. Having this level of accessibility provides prophets with a way to respond to the prediction.

We have many examples of prophets seeing on this level. It was evident in the ministry of the prophet Micaiah. He saw what God wanted to do and why He wanted to do it. Moses is again a trusted example. Again, in Exodus 5:1, he told Pharaoh God said, "Let My people go." This is where we tend to stop reading. Preachers love to preach those words. But, Moses also told Pharaoh why God wanted the people released from captivity. He said, "*...that they may hold a feast to Me in the wilderness.*"

Psychics may be able to tell you what is going to happen,

but they cannot tell you why. That is because there is a level of information that God calls "His secret." And only His servants have access to that knowledge. What good is a prophecy over your life if it does not have a context? God will tell you what He is going to do and why.

Here is scripture, which confirms that God will give us the "why" in His plans for our lives. In James 1:5-8, the author addresses a group of believers struggling with their faith during persecution. He starts off his letter to them, encouraging them to have a positive attitude about their dilemma. When he gets to verse 5, he tells them that they can ask for wisdom. Solomon defined wisdom for us in 1 Kings 3:9. He said, "Lord, give me an understanding heart." Some versions say a discerning heart. All of them communicate the same idea. Wisdom is an insightful heart. Insight is the property of seeing into something. In other words, insight helps us understand why things happen and gives us the ability to know how to apply our understanding.

For example, Abraham knew that God wanted to give him a child. He also knew why. God told the prophets He was going to punish Israel; He also said why. He also told them He was going to redeem the world. Again, likewise, He told them why He wanted to do so. Context is everything. What good is a prediction of a destructive storm if we don't know what is it means to our lives.

Kim Clement was a modern prophet that I admired. He was one of the few balanced prophets of our time. His prophecies were not always fluffy words, like those prophesying today. Sometimes he proclaimed a natural disaster to be God's judgment on man's sinful behavior. When he did, he always received massive backlash. I always respected his boldness. It takes a lot of courage to make this kind of prediction in this day. People are so convinced that Satan causes every unfortunate event and can't imagine that God has a hand in it. Yet, sometimes God is behind some of our unpleasant experiences. We, however, lack prophets with the ability to give context to God's activity.

I once told God, that I struggled to see the usefulness of a prediction meant to encourage change if no one knows that He desire the change. Someone has to give context to the events on God's calendar. The word prophet means interpreter of the oracles of God. The word interpret means to explain. That means that prophets are not only to make predictions but must also learn how to interpret those events in light of God's will. The question is not, can they see the future, but can they explain God's role in it!

There is a saying, "If a tree falls and there is no one around to hear it, does it make a sound?" Predictions without meaning are like trees falling when no one is there to hear it. Furthermore, if something divine happens and there is no one there to report it, does it really matter? Explaining the will of God is a prophet's responsibility. No psychic can do this for us. That is because they only have access to the lowest form of revelation.

Revelations of God's Heart

Now let's talk about the highest level of revelation—the revelation of God's heart. I believe that our skewed perception of God's nature is one of His biggest challenges to developing a meaningful relationship with humanity. When referring to Him, we often do so by using terms associated with inanimate objects. For instance, we call Him "it" or "the universe" or "a force." These terms communicate our view of God as a foreigner. This view often hinders our ability to see His human qualities. In fact, though the Bible clearly expresses those qualities, people allow His seemingly cruel acts to overshadow them. While He may not be human, He is definitely more like us than we let ourselves know.

We even have a mantra, Genesis 1:16, the proclamation that we are created in God's image. Nonetheless, we declare this idea while denying Him the opportunity to build a meaningful relationship with us. Please understand that God has feelings. He feels jealousy, anger, love, embarrassment, joy, displeasure, and sadness, just like us. We must understand and accept this truth. It is especially true for prophetic people. Our job is not merely to predict the plans of God. Our central role is to reveal what is in His heart—how He feels about any given situation or person.

One of the best examples comes from the life of the prophet Hosea. In my opinion, this is one of the weirdest books in the Bible. God told the prophet to marry a prostitute and have children with her. During the marriage, God allowed the woman to return to whoring several times. When she did,

God made Hosea go and spend his hard-earned money to repurchase her. Finally, Hosea prayed a hedge of protection over her, and things got better. Now, why did God put this prophet through such a gut-wrenching ordeal? God did so to help the nation of Israel see how much they had hurt His heart by serving other gods. He also wanted them to know that regardless of their behavior, He would fight tooth and nail to have them back.

I want you to notice that the emphasis of the revelation was not a prediction of a future event. Instead, the focus was on communicating God's heart and feelings. Sometimes prophets forget that God is a person. Embracing the human-like nature of God leads us to seek His heart, not the future. We need to know how God feels about a situation. I often read Ezekiel and see the prophet as a trusted place for God's heart to be heard. This is where we start seeing the most significant difference between psychics and prophets. Psychics focus on trying to predict the future. Prophets focus on communicating God's heart. Psychics cannot prophesy at this level because this level of prophetic expression requires a relationship with God.

Here is a noteworthy example in 2 Chronicles. In this chapter, King Jehoshaphat and King Ahab came together to fight against Syria. Before going to war, they sought divine counsel and turned to a group of men called prophets. Some believe they were prophets of Baal. When inquired of by these two kings, they prophesied. Let's read their words in 2 Chronicles 18:5.

> Then the king of Israel gathered the prophets together, about four hundred men, and said to them, "Shall I go against Ramoth Gilead to fight, or shall I refrain?" So they said, "Go up, for the Lord will deliver it into the hand of the king."

After hearing these words, Jehoshaphat requested to hear a prophetic word from a real prophet. While waiting for the arrival of a genuine prophet, the false prophets continued to prophesy. Here are more of their predictions.

> The king of Israel and Jehoshaphat the king of Judah, having put on their robes, sat each on his throne, at a threshing floor at the entrance of the gate of Samaria; and all the prophets prophesied before them. Now Zedekiah the son of Chenaanah had made horns of iron for himself; and he said, "Thus says the Lord: 'With these you shall gore the Syrians until they are destroyed.' " And all the prophets prophesied so, saying, "Go up to Ramoth Gilead and prosper, for the Lord will deliver it into the king's hand."

Notice the emphasis on making predictions. These limited psychics had nothing more to offer. Now while these words went forth over the kings, a prophet named Micaiah arrived. Once on the scene, the psychics tried to intimidate him to prophesy according to their words. Initially, he obliged them. I am not sure why, maybe he felt fearful, or perhaps he was being facetious. Either way, he complied. After discerning his dishonesty, king Ahab insisted that he be truthful. Look at his prophecy.

> Then he said, "I saw all Israel scattered on the mountains, as sheep that have no shepherd. And the Lord said, 'These have no master. Let each return to his house in peace.' "

This is the first part of his prophecy. It is predictive. After sharing the prophetic message, the king rebuked him. The rebuke led to a more in-depth prophetic word. Let's read his words.

> Then Micaiah said, "Therefore hear the word of the Lord: I saw the Lord sitting on His throne, and all the host of heaven standing on His right hand and His left. And the Lord said, 'Who will persuade Ahab king of Israel to go up, that he may fall at Ramoth Gilead?' So one spoke in this manner, and another spoke in that manner. Then a spirit came forward and stood before the Lord, and said, 'I will persuade him.' The Lord said to him, 'In what way?' So he said, 'I will go out and be a lying spirit in the mouth of all his prophets.' And the Lord said, 'You shall persuade him and also prevail; go out and do so.' Therefore look! The Lord has put a lying spirit in the mouth of these prophets of yours, and the Lord has declared disaster against you."

Addressing a Specific Fear

Do you see the difference between the words of the psychics and the prophet? To see it, you must ignore the visual intrigue of Micaiah's prophecy and focus on the contextual breadth and depth of his words. His prophecy tells us what is going to happen, why it is going to happen, and communicates God's feelings about the situation. Shallow prophetic words have little to no depth at all. Though the prediction may be accurate, it has no context or meaning. This goes back to the last chapter's principle # 5, Practice Precaution: Say something meaningful.

If you search the scriptures, you will find similar instances. Look at the prophecies of Isaiah, Malachi, Zachariah, and others. Notice the depth of understanding imparted by their prophecies. Their words are rich with God's heart and feelings about Israel. They were not just predictions, but predictions rooted in God's heart.

Can God Use Psychics?

One of the most puzzling things to see is psychics with a track record of accuracy. How is this possible? It is especially confusing when you consider that Deuteronomy 18:21 poses a question that God answers explicitly. Let's read it.

Verse 21 presents us with the question:

And if you say in your heart, 'How shall we know the word which the Lord has not spoken?'—

Is God Still Speaking?

Now read God's precise answer in verse 22. His response sets a standard whereby we validate a prophet's message, and ultimately his or her ministry. It reads.

when a prophet speaks in the name of the Lord, if the thing does not happen or come to pass, that is the thing which the Lord has not spoken; the prophet has spoken it presumptuously; you shall not be afraid of him.

Based on verse 22, a prophet's ministry can be justified by his or her ability to foretell with accuracy. Again, it makes us ask that question, are psychics and prophets the same? I know some of you feel as though psychics are scammers. But I want you to know that they foretell at a 50% rate of accuracy. Some may choose to see the 50% inaccuracy as a half empty glass. However, it should make you wonder how these godless persons can get it right 50% of the time. Again, for that reason, we do not use insight or foresight as markers to justify who is and is not a prophet.

To make matters more confusing, Deuteronomy 18 sets in place what we call an apparent contradiction. The contradiction, however, is going to help us answer the question at hand—does God speak to psychics. Let's read Deuteronomy 13:1-2. *(We have read this a few times, but it is necessary to reread it.)*

"If there arises among you a prophet or a dreamer of dreams, and he gives you a sign or a wonder, and the

sign or the wonder comes to pass, of which he spoke to you, saying, 'Let us go after other gods'—which you have not known—'and let us serve them,'

Notice that one passage qualifies the prophetic messenger by the accuracy of the prediction. Yet the other passage tells us that a psychic can predict the future accurately. Why is God, as we say in America, talking out of both sides of His face? How can we know the difference between genuine prophetic ministry and phony psychic experiences if both have the potential to be right? I am glad you asked the question.

First, let's look at why God says He allows this situation to happen. Deuteronomy 13:3

...you shall not listen to the words of that prophet or that dreamer of dreams, for the Lord your God is testing you to know whether you love the Lord your God with all your heart and with all your soul.

Stop what you are doing and say the word "options." The passage tells us that God gives us the option to do right. As much as we all wish evil was not in this world, the truth is it is not going away anytime soon. That being the case, we are always faced with options and choices. That is why the Tree of the Knowledge of Good and Evil was in the Garden of Eden. God always allows us to serve and obey Him. He does not assume that our allegiance is inherent. And He was right. Over and over again, both the Old and New Testament show us man's battle to do right by God. Even today, after knowing the tremendous sacrifice made for our souls, many believers still choose to do evil over good. We do so because we have options.

As it relates to the supernatural, the scriptures are full of options. There is not one supernatural expression that did not have an equally evil counterpart. For instance, Moses was a miracle worker that competed with the magicians. Daniel was a dream interpreter and advisor that competed against the wise men and soothsayers. Lastly, the prophets, such as Elijah, competed with the psychics.

Even the New Testament shows us this competitive spirit. Acts 8:9-13 tells us about the competition between Simon, the sorcerer, and Phillip the evangelist. These illustrations beg us to ask a question: If God is all-knowing and all-powerful, why is He competing with inferior spirits? Again, we must turn to the scriptures for the answer. He states His reason very clearly in the Bible. Let's read Romans 9:18.

> *For the Scripture says to the Pharaoh, "For this very purpose I have raised you up, that I may show My power in you, and that My name may be declared in all the earth."*

There it is, stated plainly. In each of our examples, one thing is common to their stories. Though they may have had to dwell and compete among the counterfeits, never once did God lose a battle. Moses showed up the magicians. Daniel outwitted the wise men. And we all know that Elijah obliterated the false prophets. Finally, we see that Phillip won a city to Jesus Christ. Likewise, in every single instance, God turned hearts to Himself. He used every competitive moment to solidify His throne in our hearts and minds.

It is also important to note that our examples capture the limited nature of Satan's kingdom. The magicians though filled with power, were limited. Moses did 12 miracles, and they could only match the first three. The wise men, though wise, were limited. They could only offer an interpretation of the king's dream if he shared it with them. However, Daniel was able to tell the dream and its meaning. The same is true with Elijah's and Phillip's example. Demonic power is limited. God's power is not.

That takes us back to the beginning of this discussion. Yes, God allows psychics access to a limited amount of power. Nonetheless, they will never be able to prophesy beyond the lowest level of revelation—predictive knowledge. This truth alone sets prophets apart from psychics.

There is Nothing to Fear

Now that you know the difference between these two gifts let peace rule in your heart. We can embrace the prophetic voice of God in our churches because there is no one like Him. Yes, Satan may try his best to mimic our Savior. Yes, he is powerful and deceptive. Still, no matter how hard he works to compete with the Risen King, he will fall short every time.

He may have power, but he is not all-powerful. Most importantly, he is not all-knowing. For that reason, he lacks access to the most important knowledge in the world; the knowledge in God's heart. Neither does he have access to God's thoughts and plans. Likewise, he cannot manifest what he does not possess. Psychics are not like prophets. Just like Satan is not like God. And the differences show in the prophecies.

8
Chapter

The Unchanging God

Now that we are in the final stretch of this book, I must ask you to ponder the question; In light of everything noted thus far, is the prophetic voice of God relevant today? I say, yes, it is. Therefore, as I close out my thoughts on the matter, I want to provide one more undisputed fact concerning the issue—God is immutable!

God's immutable nature is a pillar of our faith. Immutability means; unchanging or not capable of change. This desirable trait in the character of God tells us that He does not and cannot change. Who He is today is who He was yesterday, and will be forevermore.

The author of the book of Hebrews says it this way:

Jesus Christ is the same yesterday, today, and forevermore. (Heb. 13:8, NKJV)

Malachi also echoes this sentiment. He wrote:

"For I am the LORD. I do not change." (Mal. 3:6, NKJV)

Both writers convey God's rock-solid nature. This facet of His character teaches us two things. One, God is dependable. And two, His dependability is possible only because He is consistent. He will always abide by the principles He set in place. This truth makes every discovery regarding His nature exciting. Every time I learn something new about Him in the Bible, my heart leaps. It does so because each revelation is a building block in my understanding of how to live a kingdom life. I know that I can apply His lessons to my life and expect a favorable outcome.

As we consider this matter, think about this; Try to imagine the principle of gravity as something that varies from day today. Imagine waking up one day with your feet on the ground and then floating on the ceiling the next day. What would you do? Would you strap yourself to the bed every night? Would you nail down the furniture? More than likely, your natural inclination would move you to try to stabilize the environment. Your need for stability directly impacts your response. Likewise, knowing that God is immutable satisfies our need for security. It is this same need that makes us choose to sit on a four-legged chair over a one-legged chair.

God is consistent. His principles are also consistent. For instance, the moon will always orbit the earth. The earth will still take 365 days to orbit the sun. Children will forever be conceived by sex between a man and a woman. Trees will always be our source of oxygen. The principles that God put in place governs all of these things. Likewise, what is true about God today was true in the past and is true in the future.

It is this remarkable character trait that makes it possible to teach people how to hear His voice. As it relates to our subject, it means that the God that spoke to the prophets at various times and in various ways is still speaking today. Let's do a recap of some consistent ideas in the Bible.

- God spoke to humans in both the Old and New Testament.
- God provided a written law which He called His voice. He also spoke to prophets and select persons. This idea is true in both the Old and New Testament.
- God spoke to men and women by various means. Again, this is a consistent truth from the Old Testament into the New Testament.

If God spoke to humanity by written and oral means in both testaments, why would anyone expect the unchanging God to change now?

Now What?

In concluding, I hope that I provoked you to consider a different point of view. I also hope that I addressed this subject objectively. I know that this is a sensitive matter for many. I understand the feeling of hesitancy some have in their hearts and minds. I get it. I have seen people deceived by a voice, dream, and vision. I know that is a real fear. However, I have also witnessed many extraordinary testimonies of people whom God delivered and prospered by the various manifestations of His voice. Furthermore, the stories of blessed encounters far exceed the less favorable ones.

With all of the facts laid bare, what is the verdict? What will you choose to believe? I started this book, asking the question, 'Is someone delusional? It may have appeared by the question and the subject that I was referring to those who claim to hear God's voice. The question, however, was rhetorical. It was meant to make you ponder. After all the things I have addressed in this book, hopefully, you see the matter clearly. I have provided scripture-based teachings, addressed the most common arguments, and I've done my best to debunk bad scripture interpretations. I have given this project my all. At this point, someone is in a state of delusion. Either those of us who dare to believe God still speaks is delusional. Or, those who dare think the opposite is true. Someone is delusional. Is it you?

9
Chapter

One Last Thing

Introducing Jesus

I would hate to assume that everyone reading this is a Christian. If you are not a believer in Jesus Christ and struggle to understand the concepts of this book, you should know that this is completely normal. The Bible says that unless you are born again you cannot see or understand the things of God.

> **John 3:3**
> *Jesus replied, "Very truly I tell you, no one can see the kingdom of God unless they are born again."*

It also says that in order to have the born-again experience that a person must first believe that God exists and that He is a rewarder of those who seek Him.

Hebrews 11:6

And without faith it is impossible to please God, because anyone who comes to him must believe that he exists and that he rewards those who earnestly seek him.

Your first step toward a brand-new life is your acknowledgement of the reality and existence of God. He promises that if you do, He will reward you for seeking Him.

Your next step is to confess with your mouth and believe in your heart that Jesus Christ died on the cross for your sins so that you could enter into a glorious relationship with a welcoming God, who has been waiting for you.

Romans 10:9

If you confess with your mouth that Jesus is Lord and believe in your heart that God raised him from the dead, you will be saved.

Then you need to repent, which simply means to go the other way. Let go of the lifestyle of wickedness and turn towards righteousness. I hear you saying but how?

Acts 3:19

Repent, then, and turn to God, so that your sins may be wiped out, that times of refreshing may come from the Lord,

This is the great part. You do not have to walk the path of righteousness in your own strength. When you accept Jesus

Christ as your Lord and Savior, He gives you the Helper, the Holy Spirit. And He will do the job of inspiring in you the very nature of righteousness.

John 15:26
When the Helper comes, whom I will send to you from the Father, that is the Spirit of truth who proceeds from the Father, He will testify about Me, and you will testify also, because you have been with Me from the beginning.

God imputes or transfers to us His righteousness when we give Him our confessions of nakedness. His Spirit will fill you and empower you to live this life we call Christianity. God made him who had no sin to be sin for us, so that in him we might become the righteousness of God.

2 Corinthians 5:21
God made him who had no sin to be sin for us, so that in him we might become the righteousness of God.

Yes, it is that simple. Just say, Lord, I know I have been wrong, and I repent (I am sorry) for the life that I lived. Say Lord, I give you my weakness and my sins and I accept your forgiveness and your righteousness. Confess with your mouth, Lord I believe that Jesus Christ your only begotten Son died on the cross for my sins and was resurrected for me. Then ask Him to fill you with His Spirit and go on with your life living empowered to do right.

This next step is optional, but it is really good for you. Often, in biblical times, when a person gave their life to the Lord, deliverance was done. Deliverance is the process of casting out evil spirits that attach themselves to people. Yes, this happens. The good news is that with salvation comes healing (mental, emotional, and physical) and deliverance. If you want to go all the way follow these next simple steps.

Statement of Renunciation

Say, Devil, I renounce your presence and your hold on my life. I am now a believer in Jesus Christ and my life is now His. That means that you have no more rights to my life and I command every unclean spirit to leave me right now. Leave my emotions. Leave my mind. And leave my body. I command all illness related to your presence in my life to go with you, in Jesus name. Amen!

If you do not have a church home, then you will need to find one quickly. The Bible tells us that we should be a part of a family of like-minded people who can strengthen, encourage us, and help us to grow in the things of God.

Colossians 3:16

Let the word of Christ richly dwell within you, with all wisdom teaching and admonishing one another with psalms and hymns and spiritual songs, singing with thankfulness in your hearts to God.

One Last Thing

If you made it to the end of the process, I would like to welcome you to the family. Now, if you read this information again, I promise you it will make more sense. The kingdom of God is not a kingdom that allows one to window shop. You must to come inside to understand it for the Bible says, "TASTE AND SEE that the Lord is Good" (Psalm 34:8). You don't get to see until you first taste!

Return Home My Sons and Daughters

The first part of this chapter is designed to present the awesome Gospel of Jesus to the seeking soul. Maybe you already know Jesus but waiver in your commitment. I don't know what caused you to retreat instead of advance. I do know that the Christian walk can often challenge our sobriety. Maybe you are one of the many victims wounded by immature believers. Or, maybe you felt excluded. Or, better yet, maybe you just fell away because it just happened. Whatever the reason, please know that God is not through with you yet. He says in Jeremiah 3:14 that He is married to the backslider.

Yet again, He tells us how to get back into the race. John tells us that we can confess and repent.

> *If you confess, He is faithful to forgive you and cleanse you from all unrighteousness. (1 John 1:9, NKJV)*

Yes, you can come on home brother or sister. God has not turned His back on you. He is right where you left Him, and He is just beaming with the anticipation of your return home. Let's pray and get this right.

Father, I confess that I have walked away from your principles and went my own way. I am sorry and I ask that you forgive me. Cleanse me from all unrighteousness. Build up a spiritual hedge around me that protects me from easily falling prey to my temptations. I also ask that you awaken the gifts of service that you have put in me. Place me into Your body and empower me with a sense of purpose and direction. Father God, thank you for forgiving me.

It Will Be Alright, Prophet

This part of especially for the prophetic person who left the church. You may be part of the new online church community. In part, you left because you found it hard to be something you did not choose in a place that despises your calling. You may be frustrated, wounded, and filled with feelings of rejection. To you, I say, arise and return. Get to your watch post. Open your eyes, hear with your ears, and declare with your mouth the word of the Lord. God is still speaking. He has plenty more to say to us. Most importantly, the Bible says, "How can they hear without a proclaimer?" God needs you to get in place. He needs you to lift up your voice and share His ideas and thoughts with the world. He says, "Be not afraid of their faces. Don't worry about whether or not you have a place. You may be rejected by them, but you are not by Me!

He says, "I need you. Get on the wall, sound the alarm, and see My reward for your obedience!"

Statement of Affirmation

I am prophet _____. I am a son/daughter of the Most High God, a servant to the Lord Jesus Christ, and I am endued by His precious Holy Spirit with prophetic power to speak on His behalf. He gave me eyes to see, so I choose to open them. He gave me ears to hear, so I tune them to His loving voice. And, He put His words in my mouth. And, with my mouth, I will glorify His name and share His thoughts, feelings, and ideas with the church and the world abroad. I am proud of my calling, and I am ready to serve.

About the Author
Kevin E. Winters

Kevin has been walking with the Lord for 30 plus years. His passion is teaching believers how to achieve intimacy with God; live a purpose-filled life, walk in God's power, and how to successfully and victoriously wage spiritual warfare. He is a gifted prophetic teacher and preacher, demonstrating profound biblical insight. Most notably, many consider him a balanced source of revelation and admire his commitment to connecting deep spiritual truths to the Scriptures accurately.

He is also the author of six other books titled, *God, Is that You, Me, or the Devil*, *You Can Hear the Voice of God Clearly*, *Undefiled Greatness*, *Undefiled Greatness Journaling Workbook*, *God-Talk: The Language of Dreams and Visions*, and *God-Talk: My Dreams and Visions Journal*.

Currently, Kevin shares God's word through his online ministry. He can be heard on YouTube and Facebook sharing what God is saying and doing in the world in this hour. He also shares his heart through blogging.

By trade he is a visual artist with the Federal Government. In this capacity he serves as a lead graphic designer and illustrator.

His hobbies include making music, creating art, martial arts, and enjoying his family.

He resides in Maryland with Tanya, his wife of 19 years. Together they have four beautiful children, Autumn, Caleb, Aaron, and Noelle. He is also a long-time member of the First Baptist Church of Glenarden where he and his wife lead the Newlyweds In Discipleship ministry and serve under the leadership of Pastor John K. Jenkins, Sr.

──── **Thank you for reading this book.** ────
Here are other fantastic titles by this author.

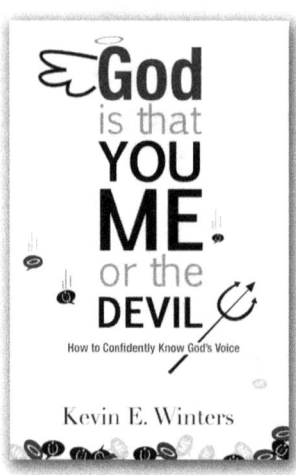

God, Is that You, Me, or the Devil?

Called a manual on the subject of hearing the voice of God, this book covers every conceivable aspect of the subject.

You Can Hear the Voice of God Clearly

"I think God is trying to tell me something." If you have ever thought that to yourself, then this is the book for you. This book teaches the believer how to hear God with clarity. It takes you from the still small voice to the clear voice of God.

God-Talk: The Language Dreams and Visions

Job 33:14-15 reveals that God like to speak to us at night, more specifically through dreams and visions. This book talks about the range of visionary experiences and teacher the reader how to decode God's language.

God-Talk: The Language of Dreams and Visions Journal

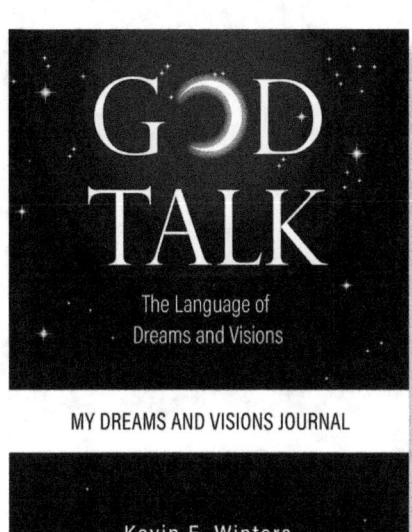

This is the perfect companion book for the God-Talk parent book. It allows you to easily record, organize, and recall your entries about your dreams and visions.

Undefiled Greatness
Harnessing the Power of Conflict to Maximize our Greatest Value
God's voice is often heard in the conflicts of life. In those moments, He uses life to reveal who we are and what we can become. This book decodes His messages and give life, victory, and direction to the human soul.

Undefiled Greatness *Journaling Workbook*
Harnessing the Power of Conflict to Maximize our Greatest Value
This is the perfect companion to the main book. This book allows you to jot down your thoughts, feelings, and expereinces in one place, so you can better analzye the voice of God through the conflicts in your life.

To hear or read Kevin's teachings visit one of the sites below.

www.facebook.com/kevinewintersministries

kevinwinters.youtube

Reach out to Kevin
kevinewintersministries@gmail.com

RECOMMENDED READING

If you are interested in learning more about hearing God's voice and prophetic ministry, here is a listing of great books to read.

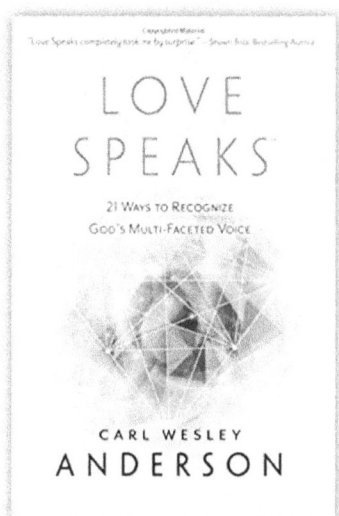
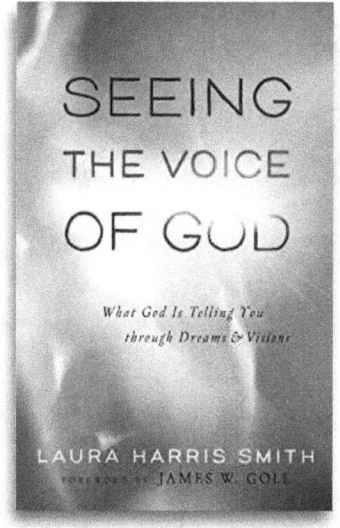

Is God Still Speaking?

www.ingramcontent.com/pod-product-compliance
Lightning Source LLC
LaVergne TN
LVHW051549070426
835507LV00021B/2479